TRADITION BY THE LAKE

A HISTORICAL OUTLINE OF
NORTH SUBURBAN SYNAGOGUE BETH EL

Morton M. Steinberg

Tradition by the Lake:
A Historical Outline of North Suburban Synagogue Beth El
Published by North Suburban Synagogue Beth El
1175 Sheridan Road, Highland Park, Illinois 60035
Copyright © 2018
By Morton M. Steinberg

ISBN-13: 978-1974695614
ISBN-10: 1974695611

Cover design by Abby Lasky.
Interior layout by Jonathan Fields.
Front cover photo from the Beth El Archives.
Back cover aerial photo by Larry Engelhart,
Deja Views Photography.

Dedicated with deep appreciation
and much love to:
Paul S. (z"l) and Sylvia (z"l) Steinberg
Miriam B. Steinberg
Joseph S. and Diane H. Steinberg
Adam, Emily, Shira and Steven
and
Naama, Leor, Max and Levi

"All Jews who are at all conscious of their identity as Jews are steeped in history."

- Sir Isaiah Berlin

CONTENTS

Seven and multiples of seven, starting with *Shabbat* on the seventh day and the Sabbatical, or seventh year, have been an important factor in the Jewish religion for millennia. According to the Aggadah, there are seventy perspectives to the Torah. Seventy elders were assembled by Moses on God's command to worship together with Aaron in the desert. According to our tradition, there are seventy different languages resulting in seventy individual nations. These are only some of the examples of the importance of seventy in our tradition.

This year two more significant meanings have been added. This is the 70th year of the establishment of the State of Israel. In our day, we have seen our people reborn in our ancient land and we can rejoice in this modern miracle. And, of course, this is the 70th year of North Suburban Synagogue Beth El. Sixteen families joined to fulfill a dream of a Conservative synagogue on the North Shore of Chicago. Fortunately for us, they took a gamble which paid off. Today we are a strong and vibrant community of over 1,000 families. We have created a second home for many people in our community where they can worship, congregate, learn and socialize together. We have exhibited leadership in the Chicagoland Jewish community and beyond. Our schools have created atmospheres for learning and educating not merely our children but also their families as well. Our involvement in education on the adult level continues to create opportunities for personal growth and a greater understanding of our tradition. Daily *minyanim*, as well as *Shabbat* and Festival services, serve as an anchor for our community and the guests who join us on special occasions. Friendships have been created, marriages have been solemnized, and significant lifetime memories have been enhanced in our halls. From birth to death, Beth El remains a home for all our members.

I have been privileged to be the Rabbi of North Suburban Synagogue Beth El for thirty of those seventy years. It has been a great honor to see children born, celebrating their b'nai mitzvah, and creating their own Jewish families. We are a place for joyous celebrations and sorrowful moments. We house events signifying our support for the State of Israel and our devotion to the worldwide Jewish community. We are proud members of the Highland Park community and our social action activities reach out with assistance to our local community and beyond.

All of this has been created by the great devotion of our staff and lay volunteers. Together we partner to build upon the vision of our founders to create an ever more exciting, vibrant and vital community. While there are many challenges ahead in our future, our 70th anniversary allows us to appreciate how far we have come even as we acknowledge how much there is yet to accomplish.

I am very pleased that we are publishing a book detailing the history of North Suburban Synagogue Beth El. I want to thank Mort Steinberg, who has spent many hours researching and writing out of love for our community and its history. I add my thanks to Rachel Kamin and Marcie Eskin of the Gray Cultural and Learning Center, who assisted with our archives and the publication of this book. Most of all, I thank the members of North Suburban Synagogue Beth El, who over the past seventy years have made our history compelling and fulfilling as they have joined together to create a *Beit Knesset* – a House of Assembly, a *Beit Midrash* – a House of Study, and a *Beit Tefillah* – a House of Worship.

May we celebrate many more anniversaries in the future.

Hazak, Hazak, VeNitchazek – May we be strong, may we be strong, and may we strengthen one another.

Rabbi Vernon Kurtz

INTRODUCTION

It would be impossible to include in this historical outline the name of every person involved in the history of North Suburban Synagogue Beth El. Many who contributed in significant ways to the unfolding story will not find their names. To them, I apologize and ask for their understanding.

This history would not have been complete without the efforts of Helen Weisel and Leonard Birnbaum, from whose prior works I have borrowed with respect to the first twenty-five years of Beth El's growth. Nor would it have been written without the efforts of the individuals who over the years served the congregation as secretary and who diligently, and often tediously, recorded the minutes of the meetings of its Board of Directors.

The primary sources for this history are the collection of minutes of the Board of Directors and the written reports of officers and various committees, as well as the thousands of published synagogue bulletins dating back to October 15, 1948. The story of Edward V. Price and the Price Estate and its acquisition by the synagogue is revealed in many newspaper articles, primarily in the *Chicago Tribune*, and in the scrapbook of Elise Weisenberger, a copy of which is in the Beth El archives. Elise was the daughter of the Price Estate gardener whose family resided in the gardener's cottage from 1911 to 1934. Of course, much of the content is based upon my own personal experiences at Beth El, beginning with my days as a child in the nursery school and continuing to the present day, as well as information gleaned from interviews with longtime members of the congregation.

I am indebted to many individuals who assisted in compiling and completing this history. Rachel Kamin, Director of the Joseph and Mae Gray Cultural and Learning Center at Beth El, first suggested publishing this history in its present form and urged me, with her characteristic enthusiasm and optimism, to do so. She and Marcie Eskin, the Librarian/Informal Education Coordinator, were totally supportive of this undertaking as well as in building the archives of the synagogue which served as an important resource for the project. Several past synagogue presidents provided significant input, including Ken Levin, Karen Kesner, Richard Schlosberg, Howard Turner and Gerald Blumberg. Also very helpful were Rabbi William Lebeau, now resident in New York City, and Beth El's next senior rabbi, Michael Schwab. Eli Krumbein, Mayer Stiebel and Rabbi Burton Cohen assisted in recalling many aspects of the early days of Beth El.

Rabbi Vernon Kurtz, with whom I have worked closely since he first came to Beth El, provided important guidance and strong support for this project, as well as much archival material which significantly enhanced the content of this volume. Rabbi Kurtz, Marcie Eskin, Rachel Kamin, Jerry Blumberg and Betsy Katz also read the manuscript and contributed valuable suggestions to improve the text.

I was fortunate to have Barbara Harrison Wohlstadter serve as the editor of this work. I am grateful not only for her professional expertise but also for her friendship. Thanks are also due to Siobhan Drummond who prepared the index and provided assistance in improving the text. I am particularly grateful to Roseann Bogusz of DLA Piper, LLP (US), who expertly typed the many versions of this manuscript. My thanks also go to Phil Feitelberg and Elliott Miller, who assisted with photographs included in this volume, and to Abby Lasky, who designed the book's cover. I also want to acknowledge the assistance of Julia Johnas of the Highland Park Public Library for her assistance in researching the history of the Edward V. Price Estate. Finally, I profusely thank my wife, Miriam, who tolerated the many long hours I devoted to this project.

In this history I have attempted to correct errors which appeared in the prior versions of this outline published by Beth El, most recently its 65th Anniversary Celebration in 2013. If any errors were not corrected, and for any new mistakes that appear in this work, I apologize to everyone whom I may have slighted.

Throughout the history of Beth El, the titles of its various officers often changed (e.g., Vice President Ritual, Ritual Vice President, etc.). I have used the titles that were attributed to individuals either in the applicable source material for the individual or in the official synagogue bylaws in effect at the time. Numerous footnotes are included in this work. For the most part, they impart facts and observations which I deemed interesting and worthy of noting, but which do not necessarily directly pertain to the history of the synagogue. Nonetheless, I believe they add interest and character to the story of Beth El and its members.

In the *Koren Yom Kippur Mahzor* (2013), Rabbi Jonathan Sacks, then Chief Rabbi of the United Kingdom, wrote:

> The greatest thing we receive from our parents and give to our children is our Jewish heritage. There are no gifts greater than these: an identity, a history, a destiny, rules to live by and ideals to which to strive. Jews and Judaism exist today because, for two-thirds of the history of humanity, Jews set it as their highest priority to hand on their faith to the next generation.

This commentary perfectly captures the spirit and intent of those who founded and built Beth El in its earliest years, as well as those who guided it over its more than seventy years of existence and those who today continue to devote so much time, effort and resources to the synagogue.

This is called an outline because it is an attempt to tell the story of Beth El essentially chronologically and non-analytically. It is told from the perspective of one who grew up in the Beth El community and who has remained a part of it. Despite that, it is truly a story of dedication, persistence and commitment, of love and devotion, to Judaism and the Jewish people. It is certainly a story of which everyone who was and is a part of it can be proud.

Morton M. Steinberg
16 Iyar 5778
May 1, 2018

I. IN THE BEGINNING
(1944–1950)

As early as 1944, perhaps even earlier, attempts had been made by traditionally minded and more observant residents of Chicago's North Shore area to organize regular religious services and to develop some type of formal religious organization.[1] Benjamin and Gertrude Harris were the leaders of this group of pioneers.[2] The Harrises maintained a Torah scroll in their house and regularly opened their home at 885 Elm Place, Glencoe, for traditional religious services. On Sunday morning March 19, 1944, and again on the following Sunday, Ben Harris hosted a small group of individuals "to discuss the organization of a Conservative Congregation on the North Shore." Those initial meetings planted the seed which eventually would grow into North Suburban Synagogue Beth El.

The end of World War II brought an increasing migration of more affluent Jewish families from traditional backgrounds to the northern Chicago suburbs of Glencoe, Winnetka and Evanston. Shortly after the end of the war, the group that had formed around the Harrises had grown to include the families of Meyer Abrams, Harry Appleman, Harold Blumberg, Isadore Braun, Miller Ehrens, Samuel Fell, Henry Fink, Alex Fisher, Louis Frohman, Max Goldberg, Seymour Graham, Joseph Gray, Allen Joseph, William Katz, Maurice Kelner, Henry Langendorf, Herman Lebeson, Arnold Natenberg, Morris Pancoe, Oscar

---

[1]   At that time, North Shore Congregation Israel, then located on Vernon Avenue in Glencoe, was the only established Jewish congregation between Chicago and Waukegan. It was one of the largest Reform "temples" in the country and maintained a strict policy against many traditional Jewish observances. It was founded in 1920 as a branch of Chicago's Temple Sinai.

[2]   Benjamin Harris was born in Poland in 1896 and studied at City College of New York and the University of Illinois. He was a partner in Epstein Reynolds & Harris, consulting chemists, and the inventor of food emulsifiers which enabled many perishables, such as mayonnaise, to be sold commercially. He was a very active and prominent Zionist.

Pinsof, Sam Reich, Max Rubenstein, Julius Salomon, Sol Shapiro and Paul Steinberg. Several of these families were members of Anshe Emet Synagogue, an established Conservative congregation on Chicago's north side. On March 8, 1945, at a meeting arranged by Ben Harris at the Glencoe Public Library, members of this group conferred with Rabbi Solomon Goldman of Anshe Emet, who expressed the desire to help establish either an independent Conservative congregation on the North Shore or an extension of Anshe Emet.

On August 27, 1946, a meeting of many members of this group was held in the home of Arnold and Stella Natenberg at 786 Greenleaf Avenue in Glencoe. At this meeting, the decision was made to organize on a formal basis, select a name, elect officers, establish regular meetings, and hold weekly services on Friday night. Arnold Natenberg was elected president of the new congregation, with Oscar Pinsof as vice president, Joseph Gray as secretary, and Seymour Graham as treasurer. The enthusiasm engendered by this decisive action quickly spread to others who saw the need for a traditionally oriented congregation in the North Shore community.

Services in those days were held on Friday nights in the homes of various members and a number of rabbis were invited to lead a *Shabbat* or special service. Soon after its formal organization, the new congregation decided to establish a regular meeting place, and a hall over the old post office on Elm Street in Winnetka was rented. Later, Friday night services were held at the Winnetka Masonic Temple. In the fall of 1946, over 300 worshippers gathered at the Winnetka Women's Club for the first High Holiday services of the new congregation. The officiating rabbi was Baruch Silverstein, a representative of the Jewish Theological Seminary of America in New York. The following year, High Holiday services were held at the same location with Rabbi Moshe Davis,[3] also from the Seminary, leading the services.

---

[3]   In 1945, Rabbi Davis (1916-1996) had been the first American to earn a doctorate at Hebrew University, Jerusalem, and would later become a leading scholar of American Jewish history.

Within a year, the new congregation sought a charter as a not-for-profit corporation and on July 18, 1947, Articles of Incorporation were issued by the State of Illinois for North Suburban Synagogue Beth El.[4] The initial officers of the new corporation were:

Arnold P. Natenberg	President
Oscar M. Pinsof	Vice President
Joseph Gray	Vice President
William M. Katz	Vice President
Harry L. Appleman	Recording Secretary
Harold R. Blumberg	Financial Secretary
Seymour Graham	Treasurer

The earliest known records of the congregation are of a special meeting of its new Board of Directors held on December 15, 1947. The secretary recorded the following directors as being present: Arnold Natenberg, Oscar Pinsof, Harry Appleman, Morris Pancoe, Max Rubenstein, Isadore Braun, Louis Frohman, Allen Joseph, Sol Sackheim, Paul Steinberg, Sam Reich, David Axelrod, Henry Fink, Phil Goodman, Herman Lebeson, Sol Shapiro and Hy Ross.

The Sisterhood was organized in October, 1947 at the Evanston home of Sarah and Isadore Braun. Mrs. Arnold Natenberg was elected its first president. That month also saw the establishment of a Sunday School, Hebrew School and Gan (nursery school), whose volunteer teachers came under the direction of the congregation's first Director of Schools, Mr. Meyer Shisler. Supervising the school program were Sarah Braun, as Sisterhood representative, and Joseph Gray, as congregation representative. Arrangements were made with the Winnetka Women's Club to use its banquet hall area for the

---

4   According to the records of the Illinois Secretary of State, the official incorporators of North Suburban Synagogue Beth El were Arnold P. Natenburg, Henry Langendorf, Oscar Pinsof, Max Goldberg, Joseph J. Gray, Seymour Graham, Morris A. Pancoe and Isadore H. Braun. All were residents of Glencoe, except Pancoe (who lived in Wilmette) and Braun (a resident of Evanston).

Sunday School; the other classes met in facilities provided at North Shore Congregation Israel in Glencoe.

The first attempts to secure a permanent home for the synagogue focused on the purchase of a large mansion overlooking Lake Michigan on Sheridan Road in Winnetka.[5] This effort was abandoned when it became evident that the synagogue's new neighbors would be inhospitable to a Jewish congregation in their midst. Shortly thereafter, the decision was made to build new facilities, away from established homes, and in 1947 a four-and-one-half-acre farm on the east side of Green Bay Road in Glencoe, at the present site of Carol Lane, was acquired for approximately $20,000. These plans changed quickly when the grounds and buildings at 1201 South Sheridan Road in Highland Park became available in the summer of 1948. (The address became 1175 Sheridan Road in 1951 when Highland Park changed its street numbering system.) However, the congregation had learned from its prior disappointment. Max Goldberg[6] was delegated to purchase the property. After numerous inspections by his "lawyers," "accountants," "brothers and sisters," etc. (i.e., the synagogue leadership), and at the urging of his wife Ida, Goldberg bought the property in his own name from Mr. Raymond Grunwald on August 18, 1948.[7]

5   Various sources indicate that this mansion property was located either in Evanston or on Harbor Street in Glencoe. However, according to a detailed written account of the early years of the synagogue prepared in 1952 by Mr. Max Goldberg and now located in the synagogue's archives, the property in fact was located in Winnetka.

6   Max Goldberg was the owner of Illinois Baking Company, a major producer of ice cream cones. According to some sources, Goldberg claimed to have invented the ice cream cone in the early 1900s. Goldberg was also a member of Rodfei Zedek synagogue in Chicago and North Shore Congregation Israel in Glencoe, and a trustee of the orthodox Hebrew Theological College in Chicago.

7   At that time the Grunwalds were in the midst of a bitter divorce, which is why Mrs. Grunwald did not sign the deed. This also explains the reason the premises were still furnished with carpeting and furniture when the congregation moved in. However, shortly after the closing of the purchase, as the congregation's leaders were taking possession of the building, Mrs. Grunwald appeared with five armed guards. At the point of a pistol, Goldberg and the others were forced to vacate "Mrs. Grunwald's one-half" of the mansion. It took some additional time for Mrs. Grunwald to vacate the home and for the synagogue to acquire her interest in the property.

The price was $147,500 plus the assumption of a $50,000 mortgage.[8] In November of that year, Max and Ida Goldberg duly transferred title to the property to the synagogue.

The new synagogue had been a lavish twenty-room residence built in 1911 by Edward Valentine Price, the founder of a successful Chicago men's clothing company.[9] Price had named the estate "Bonita Vista" because of its stunning views overlooking Lake Michigan.[10] The Price Estate was designed by Ernest Mayo, a British architect who had moved to Chicago for the 1893 World's Columbian Exposition and remained to become a well-known designer of North Shore residences.[11] It quickly became a second home to Beth El's families.[12] Dominated by a large mansion house constructed in the style of the French Renaissance, the seven acres of meticulously landscaped grounds featured a caretaker's lodge[13] with attached greenhouse, a formal garden area, a large garage/stable building with a second

[8]   The mortgage was held by Mr. Harry Kunin who had purchased the property in 1934 from the estate of Edward V. Price for only $80,000. Kunin sold it to the Grunwalds in 1945 for $125,000 when he retired to California. In the summer of 1948, a delegation of Beth El leaders, including Mr. Louis Frohman, traveled to California and met with Mr. Kunin, offering to dedicate a portion of the new synagogue in memory of his mother if he would grant concessions on the mortgage. This had no appeal to him and no concession was granted.

[9]   Ed. V. Price & Co. was located at 319 West Van Buren Street in Chicago, and its famous business motto was "Who's Your Tailor?" Price was born in Savannah, Missouri in 1854 and led an exciting life as a cowboy, stagecoach driver and silver miner in the West before moving to Chicago and founding his company in 1896. After moving to Highland Park, he became prominent in the community and was a founder of Highland Park Hospital in 1918.

[10]   In an article appearing in the *Chicago Tribune* on August 25, 1948, the mansion was described as "one of Highland Park's residential showplaces."

[11]   Mayo's designs also included Highland Park's old Hotel Moraine on Sheridan Road, the Felix Lowy House at 140 Sheridan Road in Winnetka, and the Woman's Club of Evanston.

[12]   The Price Estate had been built at an estimated cost of $750,000. Price had attempted, unsuccessfully, to sell it in 1923 and again in 1931.

[13]   The caretaker's lodge, or coach house as it is called today, was the home of the Weisenberger family, German-speaking immigrants. Albert Weisenberger was the head gardener for the estate. In the early 1920s, he hired as his assistant Angelo Pasquesi, a member of the extended Pasquesi family now prominent in many retail ventures on the North Shore.

floor apartment, an English tea house in the rear yard with a switchback pathway leading to a private beach on Lake Michigan, and a playground with adjoining tennis courts.[14] Only a long, narrow circular driveway and walkways of inlaid red Philadelphia pressed brick interrupted the acres of lawn and numerous stately trees that fronted the main house. An offering brochure prepared for the sale of the estate boasted that the residence featured:

> 22 rooms, 9 bathrooms....city water and Artesian well water. The floor in the main entrance is of Italian marble. The woodwork in the library and main dining-room is Circassian walnut, the large living-room is of mahogany and the main hallway and stairs...of oak....The porches and terraces of Welsh tile overlook the Lake....An Aeolian pipe organ costing $24,000 is installed on the second floor.[15]

The premises were ideally suited to the congregation's purposes. The bedrooms on the second floor became classrooms, the library became the rabbi's study, and the large sun parlor, complete with a fully working interior Pompeian fountain and fish pond, was converted into the sanctuary. The tennis courts became the perfect site on which to construct the congregation's *sukkah* each fall. The last service of the congregation held at the Winnetka Women's Club, on September 18, 1948, included the bar mitzvah of Avrum Gray, son of Joseph and Mae Gray. In October, Allen Rubenstein, son of Mr. and Mrs. Louis Rubenstein, became the first to celebrate his bar mitzvah in Beth El's new home.

In the fall of 1948, the congregation engaged the services of

---

14   The beach at the foot of the bluff was for many years used by the synagogue's summer day camp. During the 1960s, the pathway eroded and a wooden stairway leading to the beach was constructed behind the tea house for use primarily by Beth El's youth groups. Within a few years, the stairway weathered, was not maintained and ceased to be used.

15   The last remnant of the red brick sidewalk, in the rear of the synagogue, was removed in 2013 in connection with the extensive renovation of the Blumberg Auditorium. The Welsh tile on the rear porch, badly deteriorated more than a century after installation, was removed in 2018 and replaced with stone pavers.

its first permanent rabbi, Maurice I. Kliers.[16] Rabbi Kliers was born in Safed, Palestine, but educated in the United States. A graduate of the University of Chicago, he was ordained by the Jewish Theological Seminary of America in 1940 and had served as the rabbi of Temple Sholom in Philadelphia. That fall the congregation also engaged its first cantor, Stanley Martin, from Congregation Am Echod in Waukegan. Eager to greet their new clergy, over 170 people attended a welcoming dinner in honor of Rabbi Kliers and Cantor Martin, held at the old Ridgeview Hotel in Evanston and chaired by Joseph Gray. Under their leadership, High Holiday services were held that fall in the old Pearl Theater on First Street, between Laurel and Central Avenues, in Highland Park.[17] By then, Beth El was already a member of the Chicago Council of United Synagogue of America, one of seventeen Conservative congregations in the Chicago area. Soon a regular means of communication with the congregants was established and the Bulletin of North Suburban Synagogue Beth El, Vol. 1, No. 1, was published on October 15, 1948 – Tishrei 12, 5709. The first editor was Ruth Shapiro. Included in that premier issue, under the heading "Personalia," was the following item:

[16] Although Rabbi Kliers was clearly the first rabbi to be employed full time by Beth El, in 1947 the position initially had been offered to, and accepted by, Rabbi Samuel S. Ruderman of Temple Beth El in Fall River, Massachusetts. Rabbi Ruderman had been ordained by the Jewish Theological Seminary in 1932 and had served as a Naval chaplain in World War II. While stationed at Great Lakes Naval Station in North Chicago, he consulted with and befriended the founding leaders of the congregation. The December 15, 1947 minutes of the Board of Directors indicate that funds were authorized to purchase a house for Rabbi Ruderman. However, shortly thereafter, under pressure from his family, he withdrew his acceptance and remained in Massachusetts. He passed away in 1968. I am indebted to Ora Beth Levine, Rabbi Ruderman's daughter and a resident of Northbrook, Illinois, who brought this episode to my attention.

[17] The following spring, one congregant, who had resigned because of his dissatisfaction with this location for religious services, demanded a refund of his dues. The Board wisely refused. In the fall of 1949, the congregation had difficulty locating a place for the anticipated 900 worshippers for High Holiday services. Samuel Meyers, proprietor of the Glencoe Theater on Vernon Avenue (now the site of an apartment building), offered his establishment but noted that its use on Kol Nidre evening would "entail some difficulty" due to the movie being shown. The House Committee was finally able once again to obtain the use of the Pearl Theater.

Our heartiest Mazel Tov to Mr. and Mrs. Harold Blumberg on the birth of their son, Gerald.

The fall of 1948 was a difficult yet exciting time for the Jewish people everywhere as they struggled to cope with the consequences of the Holocaust in Europe and to build the new State of Israel. Along the North Shore, the founders of Beth El also faced many challenges, frequently financial, that would continue for several years until a more solid fiscal foundation was established. But this was also a time to dream of the future and to build for the sake of their children and the community. What stood out above all the pains of growth were the intense devotion to the congregation and the astounding dedication of congregants to assure that Beth El would survive and prosper. Throughout these difficult times, one voice was constantly raised, not only to direct the course of the synagogue and to provide encouragement and leadership, but also to raise the funds, boost the morale and help implement the solutions. Harold Blumberg, among the founding families of Beth El, was one of the most active leaders of the synagogue in its first years of struggle and he would continue to be the key lay leader of the congregation throughout the 1950s and well into the following decade.

Shortly after moving into its new home, the congregation's leadership approved a budget of $67,223.40 but soon realized that its annual dues of $100 per family were inadequate to cover the many needs of the synagogue. At the *Kol Nidre* service on Yom Kippur that fall, the lay leadership of the congregation felt compelled to hold a fundraising appeal which included the calling of names, a procedure which resulted in more than a few complaints. Benjamin Harris, in a letter to a disgruntled congregant, explained the reasons and rationale for the appeal: "Under the circumstances, the Board of Directors feel that no offense was committed and that the situation, that is to say the extremely pressing needs of the congregation, warranted the steps that were taken." But still the funds raised failed to meet the financial requirements of the synagogue. In

November, 1948, the congregation borrowed $27,000 from the Belmont National Bank in Chicago, but only after the loan was personally guaranteed by individual officers and directors of the synagogue. The following year, a portion of the south section of lawn, which had once been an extensive vegetable garden, was turned into a needed parking lot and a new driveway was installed to permit cars to exit the property more easily, but funds available were insufficient to pay the contractor, Sydney Mayer. He patiently agreed to wait for payment.

Although faced with fiscal difficulties, the new congregation's programs flourished as Beth El was becoming known in the greater Chicago community.[18] In December, 1948, Rabbi Oscar Fasman, president of the Hebrew Theological College, and Rabbi Ralph Simon of Congregation Rodfei Zedek were official guests at the new synagogue. At the formal installation of Rabbi Kliers, celebrated the weekend of April 8-9, 1949, Rabbi Solomon Goldman of Anshe Emet officiated along with Rabbi Jacob Weinstein of Temple K.A.M. and Rabbi Edgar Siskin of North Shore Congregation Israel.

Fulfilling a need for its young people, eighty boys and girls attended the Jewish Youth League for high school students in joint programming with North Shore Congregation Israel; the group's leader was Robert Asher. Younger boys were active in the synagogue's Tephilin Club. For college-aged students and post-college graduates, a Young People's Club was organized and Arthur Pancoe was elected its first president; in October, 1948, the group held its first dance at the new synagogue. In December, the new synagogue hosted its first Leaders Training Fellowship (LTF) Kinus; over fifty high school students from the Midwest, members of the LTF youth organization newly formed under the auspices of the Jewish Theological Seminary, sleeping on cots set up in the second-floor bedrooms, met for study and fellowship. Early in 1949, the Men's Club was founded with Har-

---

[18] In April, 1949, as the magnitude of the Holocaust was becoming known generally and at the urging of Maurice Kelner, who had guaranteed to cover all costs, the Board of Directors approved bringing Rabbi Andor Breuer, a Holocaust survivor, from Europe to serve as an assistant to Rabbi Kliers for two years. Inexplicably, he never accepted this offer.

old Heisler as its first president; its goals were to promote the general welfare of the congregation, sponsor youth activities and "foster good fellowships among our members." On June 12, 1949, the Men's Club held its first Fathers', Sons' and Daughters' Picnic on the synagogue grounds. It was the forerunner of what would later become an annual Sports Night event for the Men's Club. That summer, Beth El also started its own summer day camp, a program which continues to the present.[19]

Tom and Lydia Bruecks served as the resident custodian, housekeeper, handyman, caterer, deputy sheriff and friend to all congregants. Tom also drove the small green school bus with the words "N.S.S. Beth El School" painted on the side. It had been a gift from the Sisterhood, one of its many generous gifts that benefited Beth El's educational programs.

Education was always a priority with the young congregation. For the most part, the supervision of this aspect of the synagogue had been under the direction of the Sisterhood, with some involvement by representatives of the Board of Directors. However, the schools operated at a deficit, which was not well received by the already financially strapped Board and which caused much consternation among the leadership of the congregation. Also, enrollment was growing rapidly and the school program needed full-time attention. To address these problems, the Sisterhood recommended that the running of the schools be delegated to an autonomous Board of Religious Education. This suggestion was adopted on August 4, 1949, at the same time that Mr. Harry Hershman, at the urging of Rabbi Kliers, was engaged as the new Educational Director.[20] In November, a twelve-member School Board was officially established with responsibility for all formal and informal educational programs. This was a true milestone in the building of the congregation. In ensuing years, the School Board (later the Board of Education) would bring an

19   The professional responsible for the day camp as well as the nursery school was Sylvia Brenner, affectionately called "Aunt Sylvia" by the children in those programs.

20   Hershman had served as educational director at Rabbi Kliers' former congregation in Philadelphia.

independent, focused approach to the development of educational programming at the synagogue. It would attract leading educators to serve the synagogue and would produce from among its membership some of the more outstanding individuals who would become leaders of the entire congregation.

Rabbi Kliers had a vision for the future of Beth El. In Beth El's first Annual Report, issued in September, 1949, he shared his goals for the young congregation:

> To build an American Jewish Community that is vital, dynamic, rich and meaningful...to generate the highest ideals of Judaism with the best ideals in Americanism... to enable our children to share Jewish experiences with a sense of joy, appreciation and creativeness...The road ahead is not an easy one....However, with the progress and promise shown thus far, we are confident of victory.

But the relationship between Rabbi Kliers and the congregation at times proved troublesome, aggravated by the precarious financial condition of the synagogue. The congregation provided him, his wife Florence, and their two children with housing, but this was in the apartment above the garage at the northwest corner of the synagogue grounds. It sorely needed repairs and although he was often promised assistance, it was not forthcoming.[21] The young congregation, which had reached a membership of 250 families by the spring of 1949, hardly had sufficient funds to pay the rabbi's annual salary and the main synagogue building required constant renovations.[22] Fundraising was a constant topic at each meeting of the Board. A donation of $300 was considered such a major gift that it was prominently mentioned in the official minutes. In June, 1949,

---

[21]   In February, 1949, the directors recognized the urgent need to improve the rabbi's housing, but money was so scarce that the Board even rejected Cantor Martin's request for $150 to enable him to attend the Cantorial Assembly meeting in New York.

[22]   In April 1949, $250 had to be spent to repair the roof of the synagogue. This was the first of what would become an almost annual expense of the congregation.

after much discussion, the directors voted by secret ballot seventeen to seven to buy a house for the rabbi at a cost not to exceed $30,000, provided that Rabbi Kliers first obtained a $10,000 loan from congregants as the down payment. This never happened. Finally, in the fall of 1949, the Board agreed to spend $4,000 to renovate the coach house and the rabbi agreed to move there.

But the tensions between the rabbi and many congregants continued. Some complaints centered on the lack of attendance at religious services and the need to improve them.[23] During the summer of 1949, the contract of Meyer Shisler, the popular Director of Schools, had not been renewed due to "friction" between him, the rabbi and members of the School Committee. Almost one-third of the synagogue's membership left with Mr. Shisler.[24] Also, the need for funds being so great, the Board again approved, over the objection of Rabbi Kliers, the holding of an appeal for funds at *Kol Nidre* services that fall, which raised $7,500.

The strain between the pulpit and the laity culminated at the Board of Directors meeting in January, 1950. Contrary to the recommendation of the Ritual Committee, the Board of Directors decided not to renew the rabbi's contract beyond June of that year. A search committee was immediately appointed by President Natenberg. That summer, Rabbi Kliers left the congregation to serve South Side Hebrew Congregation in Chicago. His last official act at Beth El most likely was officiating at the wedding of Elaine Frohman and Eliezer Krumbein on June 18, 1950.[25] On August 20 of that year, Arnold and Stella Natenberg's daughter Phyllis celebrated her wedding in the syna-

---

23   In this vein, at the request of Benjamin Harris and Joseph Gray on behalf of the Ritual Committee, the Board in February 1949 approved as an "experiment" the use of an organ at religious services. This practice continued until the mid-1960s, when the organ literally broke down and the more traditionally minded leadership of the congregation at that time decided not to repair it.

24   Mr. Shisler went on to a long, honorable and distinguished career in Jewish education at North Shore Congregation Israel in Glencoe. He died in 1995.

25   At that time, Eli Krumbein was the director of Religious Education at North Shore Congregation Israel.

gogue's first outdoor ceremony, held in the formal gardens on the north side of the Price Estate; Rabbi Goldman of Anshe Emet Synagogue officiated.

At its annual meeting in June, 1950, the congregation presented Arnold Natenberg with a specially commissioned portrait of himself to hang in the synagogue in recognition of his years of service as the founding president;[26] Harold Blumberg was then elected as the new president.[27] Over 300 people attended the meeting, which was followed by a barbeque supper and dance on the synagogue's beautiful and extensive lawn.[28] In the fall of 1950, with a membership roster of 288 families, Rabbi Joel Geffen of the Jewish Theological Seminary in New York was engaged to lead the High Holiday services for the Beth El families, who worshiped in a large tent erected on the synagogue grounds since other facilities were unavailable. A professional choir led by Maurice Nev was engaged for the first time to assist in the services. On Friday evening, October 20, Beverly Joyce Rubenstein (later Dratler), the sister of Allen Rubenstein whose bar mitzvah two years earlier was the first celebrated in the synagogue's new home, became the first girl to celebrate her "bas" mitzvah at Beth El.[29]

But the financial stress continued. The congregation had never paid the contractor who the year before had constructed the

[26] The portrait disappeared mysteriously in July, 1952. It was never recovered. Since 1990, photographs of all congregational past presidents, including Natenberg, have been on permanent display in the main corridor of the synagogue.

[27] An avid equestrian, Blumberg regularly rode horses for recreation and the Blumberg family was the owner of Venetian Way, the winner of the 1960 Kentucky Derby. In the 1950s, Blumberg's parents, Mr. and Mrs. Isaac Blumberg, donated to Beth El the oil painting "The Wailing Wall" by artist Adolf Gelff which for many years was displayed above the fireplace in the living room of the Price mansion. It now is displayed in the Gamze Galley in the sanctuary building.

[28] During the summer of 1950, the House Committee reported to the Board on two recent "outstanding events" held by the growing membership at the synagogue: The Frohman Wedding and the Pinsof "Bar Metzvah (sic)."

[29] Interestingly, Rabbi Philip L. Lipis officiated at that service. He coincidentally had been invited to speak at the synagogue that *Shabbat* by the congregation's Rabbi Replacement Committee.

new parking lot and driveway. In June, 1950, the Board agreed to sell to him the vacant land in Glencoe which it still owned for the discounted price of $18,000, thereby settling an outstanding debt and also realizing needed cash. Although by the end of July the congregation had $646.38 in its bank account, the financial vice president forecast a deficit in excess of $11,000 for the coming year. Nonetheless, the determination and vision of the Board remained unshaken. In the fall, the Board voted overwhelmingly to construct new facilities for the growing congregation, but only when adequate funds became available.

II. BUILDING A CONGREGATION (1950–1969)

On December 7, 1950, at a meeting attended by twenty-three members of the Board of Directors despite an unusually severe snow storm, David Axelrod, chairman of the Rabbi Replacement Committee, recommended the selection of Rabbi Philip L. Lipis of Oakland, California to serve as Beth El's second spiritual leader. In searching for a new rabbi, the committee had sought an individual who would serve as a "preacher, pastor, educator and spokesman of the Jewish community" for the growing congregation. In its six-page report, the committee recounted its interviews[30] with thirteen candidates and stated its reasons for unanimously recommending Rabbi Lipis:

> The committee believes that Rabbi Lipis, on the basis of his background and qualifications, and our having met with him and also Mrs. Lipis, have [sic] found in him a Rabbi whom [sic] we believe is not only most effective in each of these [above-mentioned] activities, but who may very well excel in each of them. [He possesses] a desire and aggressiveness to build our synagogue, with us, in accordance with our aims.

Rabbi Lipis was born in Tiraspol, Russia in 1906 and came to this country in 1913. A graduate of City College of New York, he was ordained by the Jewish Theological Seminary in 1930. After studying in Palestine at the Hebrew University and the Yeshiva of Rav Kook, he pursued graduate studies at Columbia University and Dropsie College. Prior to becoming the spiritual leader of Temple Beth Abraham in Oakland, California, he had been the rabbi of congregation Beth El in Camden, New Jersey. During

---

30   The committee's initial interview with Rabbi Lipis took place at the home of Meyer Abrams. Years later, Arthur Frohman recalled "the Rabbi's enthusiastic entrance and greeting" and the "verve and positiveness" with which he answered questions, "and he didn't even have Shoshanah along!"

World War II, he served for three years as a chaplain in the U.S. Navy, stationed first in Guam and later with the Marines in the New Hebrides (now known as Vanuatu). In correspondence with Harold Blumberg prior to the committee's recommendation, Rabbi Lipis wrote:

> For years I have been searching to identify my life and work with the life and activity of a young, vital congregation, genuinely, even passionately, desirous of making Judaism a dynamic force in their lives and the lives of their young. I am impressed that your congregation offers such a rich opportunity.

The committee's recommendation was accepted and carried by the unanimous vote of the Board of Directors. Rabbi Lipis led his first service at Beth El on February 9, 1951. The following month, on March 10, he officiated at the bar mitzvah of Laurie Benjamin, son of Mr. and Mrs. Irwin Benjamin, the first of hundreds he would conduct over the course of his tenure at Beth El. The rabbi's formal installation was held on June 24. Rabbi Solomon Goldman of Anshe Emet Synagogue was accorded the honor of installing the new rabbi. [31]

Rabbi Lipis infused the entire congregation with his spirit and energy. One of his first innovative programs was to organize a community seder on the second night of Passover at the old Hotel Moraine on Sheridan Road in Highland Park. It was attended by 236 people! On April 15, 1951, at an afternoon *mincha* service, the congregation dedicated its first memorial tablet [32] to commemorate the *yahrzeit* of departed loved ones and later that year it published its first Memorial Booklet. By July, 1951, 311 families appeared on the membership roster and Membership Chairman Harvey Yormark was work-

---

[31]   Shortly after his arrival, Rabbi Lipis ordered the Pompeian fountain and fish pond removed from the sanctuary following the appearance of an article in a local publication characterizing Beth El as the only synagogue with its own "baptismal font."

[32]   This tablet, memorializing Sieg Natenberg and sixteen other departed souls, is permanently located in the Sager Bet HaMidrash.

ing tirelessly to increase that number. One innovation of his committee was the sponsorship of a series of afternoon teas at the synagogue for prospective members who would have the opportunity to meet the rabbi, cantor and educational director of the congregation in an informal setting, and "to enjoy the warmth and friendliness for which Beth El is known." That summer the congregation established the Beth El Forum Series. Designed to bring outstanding speakers on interesting and varied topics to the North Shore, its programs were generally held at the Winnetka Community House. This was an enormously successful and popular program that continued for many years. In September, 1951, the congregation accepted the gift of two large candelabra from brothers Herman and Maurice Spertus in memory of their father Harry Spertus, which were in use in the small sanctuary, later to be known as the Sager Bet HaMidrash, until its renovation in 2017. [33]

In 1951, the Ritual Committee, under Maurice Kelner's direction, arranged for High Holiday services to be held at the Highland Park Recreation Center and afterward received the commendation of the Board "for the beauty and dignity" of these services.[34] The "Rec" Center, later known as the Karger Center, would continue as the synagogue's High Holiday home through 1956. 1951 was also the year that Rabbi and Shoshanah Lipis invited the entire congregation to their home (they were then residing in the coach house) on the second day of Rosh Hashanah. Their High Holiday "open house" continued as an annual event throughout their tenure at Beth El.

The rapid growth in the number of youngsters in the school program filled the synagogue's facilities to capacity. The 1951-52 school year began with eighty-eight children enrolled in the

---

[33]   Herman Spertus left the congregation within a few years, but Maurice Spertus remained an active member of the congregation until he passed away in 1986. Both brothers were instrumental in the establishment and growth of the Spertus Institute in Chicago. Herman passed away in 2006 at the age of 105.

[34]   To emphasize the dignity and solemnity of the *Kol Nidre* service, Rabbi Lipis and President Blumberg recommended that officers and directors attend dressed in tuxedos.

Hebrew School and 321 in the English-language Sunday School. Jonas Meyers reported to the directors that the School Board "has considered the use of the dining room, the library, the back porch, the garage, and the stable" for classrooms. Ultimately, arrangements were made for classes to be held on Sundays at the nearby Ravinia Public School,[35] but it was clear that the growing Jewish population in the northern suburbs was fueling the rapid growth of the synagogue and that significant expansion was not only desirable, but also essential to the continued success of the congregation.

With the rabbi's strong encouragement, the Executive Committee in August, 1951 recommended that "the Board undertake a Capital Fund Campaign in the amount of $300,000 to provide the means for a Sanctuary, School Building, Social Center, and for the retirement of the mortgage on our property." President Harold Blumberg promptly appointed a committee to assist in broadening the base of contributors and also a Building Commission to "work out plans for a Building Program." The initial chairman of the Building Commission was the respected former president Arnold Natenberg.

Religious services were not ignored by the Board. The new rabbi attracted many new regular worshippers to Beth El, but he firmly, although diplomatically, refused to allow the Board to dictate the religious practices that would be followed. During his first year at Beth El, he informed the Board that the pulpit is his responsibility, but he would gladly listen to recommendations from and consult with the Ritual Committee on all matters. By early 1952, the rabbi announced that in response to numerous requests from members who needed to say *kaddish*, a daily *minyan* at 7:30 a.m. and again at 7:30 p.m. would be instituted "with the intention to make these arrangements permanent." He also laid the groundwork for instituting a regular Junior Congregation on Saturday mornings. By the first anniversary of Rabbi Lipis' tenure at Beth El, President Blumberg could announce that

35   On December 23, 1951, the school children presented a special "Chanukah" program at the Ravinia School Auditorium, featuring Judy Perlman singing the Hebrew song "Haneyros Halalu."

the sanctuary was almost always filled for Friday night services.[36]

Rabbi Lipis also took an active role in the educational programs at Beth El, teaching several classes himself. In 1952, he announced that he had formed the first "Bas Mitzvah" class at the synagogue, consisting of three girls,[37] and two years later he would form a Bat Mitzvah Club to provide a youth activity for girls similar to the boy's Tephilin Club. He also announced that beginning in 1953 the requirement for completion of the confirmation course would be increased by one additional year of study. (As a result, there was no confirmation class of 1953!) His attention was also focused on adult education. That year he organized four Home Study Groups, based on his experience in Camden, New Jersey. He also organized two "Institutes," one for Passover and one for "Chanukah," the purposes of which were to help congregants "learn thru [sic] song and story, diet and ritualism, decoration and explanation," ways of making these holidays more meaningful in their homes. In recognition of these accomplishments, the directors unanimously passed an extraordinary resolution on February 7, 1952, expressing their "appreciation and deep thanks for the fine aggressive spirit... and zeal with which [Rabbi Lipis] has organized commendable projects... [and obtained] cooperation from all members," and proclaiming that they were "proud to have him as their spiritual leader."

One of the first decisions by the new Building Commission, made in January, 1952, was to select Isadore Braun, a founder of the congregation, as the architect for the three new facilities intended to be constructed. The likelihood of success for this ambitious project increased as fundraising efforts continued over the winter months. By April, 1952, over $72,000 in pledg-

---

[36]   Rabbi Lipis was not adverse to innovations in encouraging attendance at services. For the evening of January 4, 1952, when he would be out of town, he announced that services would be chanted by "Cantor Harold Blumberg" and led by "Rabbi Benjamin R. Harris." There was a large turn-out for that special service.

[37]   It is likely that the three girls were Marsha Lanyi (later Caspi), Sidra DeKoven (later Ezrahi) and Barbara Lerner (later Spectre), all of whom would make *aliyah* to Israel and have a significant impact in politics and Jewish education in that country.

19

es had been received and cash receipts were placed into a special account at the Glencoe National Bank. The Board refused to permit those funds to be used for daily operations, even in the face of an anticipated operational deficit of $8,000. To cover the deficit, the Board authorized billing the amount of the deficit equally among all of the members of the congregation: the first "special assessment" at Beth El. That June, dues were increased by a startling thirty percent: from $100 to $130 per family.

In April, 1952, the congregation finally had an opportunity to share the vision of the Board and its architect for the future development of its facilities. Seymour Graham, Secretary, recorded in the minutes: "Mr. Isadore Braun unveiled the picture showing the New Building. Everyone was thrilled...and hoped that this dream would someday become a reality." But by June it was apparent that the entire construction plan adopted the prior year could not be built for the $300,000 originally anticipated. Accordingly, at the suggestion of Joseph Horwitz, the Board authorized the Building Commission to proceed initially with the construction of only the school building at a cost of $206,000. William Balkin was designated the chairman of the cornerstone-laying ceremonies. September 14, 1952 was a bright and sunny day. The congregation, young and old, gathered near the site of the new construction to celebrate this historic undertaking by the young synagogue. After speeches by Balkin, Rabbi Lipis, Harold Blumberg and other dignitaries, including Rabbi Siskin from North Shore Congregation Israel, former president Arnold Natenberg and others "helped" apply the mortar to the school's first bricks as an engraved marble slab, imported from Israel for the occasion, was carefully placed into position by workmen. That marble slab, in its original position, is still visible in the school building.[38]

Amidst the excitement generated by the prospects of new construction and expanded facilities, synagogue life flourished.

---

[38] As a memento of the occasion, each donor received a small metal trowel with a wooden handle affixed with an engraved plaque reading: North Suburban Synagogue Beth El School Building Dedication September 14, 1952.

Men's Club [39] and Sisterhood, providing important social programs as well as service projects, grew rapidly. A group of thirty-five young couples organized the Young Married Group, which quickly grew under the leadership of Herb Gritton (and which became the Mr. and Mrs. Club a few years later). The Sisterhood, anticipating the new construction, produced a plan to raise funds by selling off the plants and shrubs in the formal gardens where the new school building would be located. That summer, in one of the first of almost identical debates held annually thereafter, the Board of Directors engaged in an intense discussion concerning a choir for the forthcoming High Holidays: Seymour Gumbiner introduced a motion to spend $2,000 on a professional choir; Jack Borkan led the opposition by moving to dispense with the choir altogether. This being a highly sensitive issue, a secret written ballot was taken: the vote was twelve opposed to a choir, eleven for it. But immediately thereafter, an anonymous Board member moved to reduce the cost for a choir to $1,000. A new vote was taken and this time the choir won by a vote of twelve in favor, eleven opposed!

In the spring of 1952, Irwin Benjamin, on behalf of the House Committee, announced the resignation of housekeepers Tom and Lydia Bruecks. They were succeeded by Morris and Lucille Byrd.[40] In the fall of 1952, Sam Reich, Vice President of Ritual, informed the Board that Cantor Martin had requested to be relieved of his contract following the High Holidays. The Board reluctantly approved this request and Cantor Martin formally departed Beth El on April 1, 1953.[41] After a search by the Ritual Committee, the Board, in April, 1953, approved its recommendation to engage Jordan H. Cohen, cantor at Am Echad congregation in Chicago. Cohen was a fourth-generation cantor and

---

[39]   The list of officers and directors of the Men's Club for 1952-53 was replete with many future leaders of the congregation, emphasizing one of the important roles that organization has played over the years in synagogue life. The list included Irwin Smith, Eli Field, Harry Young, Herman DeKoven, Milton Leeds, Ben Sager and Joseph Horwitz.

[40]   The initial replacements were Mr. and Mrs. Henry DeVroeg, who began work on Monday, April 7 and quit, for unexplained reasons, on Tuesday, April 8.

[41]   Cantor Martin left to go into the business of selling insurance.

son of the renowned Cantor Tevele Cohen of Chicago. His first service at Beth El was on May 22, 1953. Cantor Cohen soon became a much beloved member of the community and would serve Beth El faithfully for the next sixteen years.[42] With the arrival of Cantor Cohen, the Lipises purchased the residence at 1154 Lincoln Avenue South, moving from the coach house which had been made available to them when they first moved to Highland Park. Cantor Cohen and his family then moved into the coach house.

In the fall of 1952, with construction progressing on the new school building, collections on pledges for the building fund were slow and funds were inadequate to pay the contractor. Harold Blumberg was able to arrange for a $50,000 mortgage loan from the Oak Park Bank at 5% interest. This was unanimously approved, along with the proposal to postpone the second and third phases of the building project (i.e., the community center and new sanctuary) until funds were available.[43] By the spring of 1953, the new school building was already in use, although still not 100% completed.[44] Enrollment had reached 435 students. On May 17, 1953, Beth El held its first Annual Dinner Dance at the Terrace Casino in the Morrison Hotel in Chicago. Chaired by Charles Podolsky, Saul Pohn and Jack Borkan, it successfully raised funds "to supply and equip the new School Building." The formal dedication ceremony for the new building was held on September 20, 1953. It was organized by William Katz and included remarks by Rabbi Siskin and the Mayor of Highland Park, Gordon Humphrey. The

---

[42] Sometime after Cantor Cohen arrived, Rabbi Lipis changed the official pronunciation of Hebrew taught at the school and used in the religious services of the congregation from *Ashkenaz* to *Sepharadit*.

[43] At about this time, Jack Borkan proposed expanding the existing sanctuary (now the Sager Bet HaMidrash) into the living room (now the Maxwell Abbell Library) by breaking down the wall between those two rooms. Although the proposal was defeated, for years afterwards that wall was called the "Borkan Wall."

[44] The kindergarten classrooms in the new school featured a Hebrew language greeting inlaid in the tile floor. Some of the *balabatim* of the synagogue felt this was sacrilegious, but Rabbi Lipis, recounting how synagogues in ancient Israel had Hebrew letters in their mosaic floors, assured them this practice was perfectly acceptable.

following spring, on June 2, 1954, Rabbi Lipis proudly oversaw Beth El's first elementary Hebrew School graduation held at the synagogue. The ceremony for the large confirmation class was held on June 13 at Edgewood School in Highland Park.

By 1953, membership in the congregation had grown to 347 families. Beth El, under steady leadership for the past two years, had weathered its initial financial storms and had expanded to meet its most serious need for classrooms. As a result, there was little controversy in the operations or direction in which the congregation was headed. This, perhaps, was the reason that attendance at meetings of the directors often dwindled to less than a quorum. In February, 1954, only eighteen out of fifty members of the Board showed up for its regular meeting. Of course, a committee was appointed to deal with this problem and soon Herman DeKoven made a recommendation to change the by-laws to address this situation.

By 1954, William Balkin, Membership Chairman, reported a membership of 403 families. That year, the Annual Dinner Dance, under chairman Albert Dolin, featured an ad book – it raised $25,000, and for many years thereafter the Ad Book Dinner Dance became an annual event of great importance, serving not only a financial need but also as an important social function. In May of that year the congregation was invited to attend the first original Beth El musical production, "Three in a Hammock," at Elm Place School in Highland Park. It was produced by the Mr. and Mrs. Club, which donated the entire proceeds of $1200 to the Building Fund.

In June, 1954, the Congregational Nominating Committee selected Edward Glazier as the new president, but in recognition of the important role the outgoing president had played, it also created a new position of Chairman of the Board for Harold Blumberg. For Rosh Hashanah services that year, Arnold Miller was engaged as the congregation's music director and organist, a position he would hold for twelve years. Although membership in the congregation had risen to 432 members, the financial situation, while tolerable, had not been totally resolved.[45] The new school building, as well as the classrooms in the original mansion building, were filled to capacity with approximately 500 students, so much so that Leonard Zieve, chairman of the School Board, announced that to alleviate over-crowding, Hebrew classes would be held on Saturday mornings. He also noted that the School Board was having success in reducing the annual deficit in the school budget "due primarily to the expansion of our Gan Department, which, aside from our Summer camp, is the only profitable department of our Beth El Schools." It was a prescient observation that would prove to be true throughout Beth El's history.

That fall also saw the real beginnings of the Beth El library, which would grow into one of the most extensive collections of any Conservative synagogue in the country. President Glazier officially appointed Sarah Braun, wife of architect Isadore Braun, and Becky Hershman, wife of the educational director Harry Hershman, as co-chairs of the "temporary" Library Committee. They, with assistance from many other women in the congregation, most notably Ruby Blumberg, Betty Benson and Rose Belloff, cataloged all the library's books and acted as volunteer librarians for many years until professional assistance was needed to take care of the burgeoning collection.[46]

The congregation now directed its attention to continuing its original plan for the enlargement of its facilities. A new Building Fund Commission, with Harold Blumberg as its chairman, recommended to the Board of Directors that a $400,000 Building Fund Campaign be undertaken to provide for a new "appropriate Sanctuary and Auditorium, and pay up the existing $53,000 deficit." The proposal was approved by a vote of thirty-three to one. By December, 1954, the campaign had received pledges totaling $240,000.

[45] In October, 1954, the Board was advised that Goodman Book Store was about to sue the synagogue for the cost of prayer books purchased in 1952 and not paid for. It immediately and unanimously authorized payment.

[46] According to Sarah Braun, Beth-El's first professional librarian was Dr. Dora Edinger, who served for approximately ten years. Dr. Edinger had trained in Europe under Dr. Leo Baeck and had worked with Martin Buber and Franz Rosenzweig at the Frankfurt Lehrhaus. By 1963, she had built the library's collection to more than 2,500 volumes.

In April, 1955, the Building Commission (separate from the Building Fund Commission, which was a fundraising effort), under the chairmanship of Allen Gellman, was authorized "to study the need for any new or modernization of old structures, alterations, furnishings, [and the] employment of [an] architect or contractor." Later that month, the Building Commission entered into a contract with Isadore Braun to design plans for a "Community Center" and "Synagogue." In May, Leonard Zieve proposed the establishment of a semi-independent group to oversee the activities of the growing youth component of the congregation. Analogous to the School Board, the Youth Commission would have representatives from the congregation, Sisterhood, Men's Club, and Mr. and Mrs. Club, its own budget, and the authority to hire professional youth leaders. With strong support from Rabbi Lipis, the proposal was approved by the Board of Directors. The first Youth Director was Steven Cohen.

Despite the many initiatives being undertaken at the synagogue, attendance at Board meetings and participation by congregants in many activities continued to be disappointingly low. There were a few new faces,[47] but overall participation was so low that Rabbi Lipis suggested the creation of an "honorary board" to meet "when warranted" as a way of both maintaining the loyalty of senior members and encouraging younger leaders to come forward. This was the start of the concept of the Board of Trustees, which would be formally established at the next annual meeting of the congregation on December 14, 1955.[48]

At a special meeting of the directors held on August 28, 1955, plans for the new construction were unveiled and open for discussion. The plans included a community center overlooking Lake Michigan and a design for a square-shaped sanctuary

---

[47] Names such as Morris Lederman, Mel Stark, Herman Finch, Nate Paset, Bernard Zell, Bud Rueckberg and Leo Carlin begin to appear frequently during this period in the Board's minutes.

[48] The first trustees of Beth El were: Harold Blumberg, chairman; Isadore Braun, Louis Frohman, Max Goldberg, Seymour Graham, Joseph Gray, Benjamin Harris, Allen Joseph, Oscar Pinsof, Samuel Reich, Max Rubenstein, Solomon Shapiro and Maurice Kelner.

topped with a dome. Once again, Harold Blumberg spoke forcefully about the need to raise funds in order to turn this dream into a reality. Enthusiasm ran high. The plan[49] was approved. A formal groundbreaking ceremony for the first phase of the plan, the community center, was held on November 27, 1955, under the chairmanship of Albert Dolin.[50] In addition to customary messages delivered by the rabbi and lay leaders, student representatives from the synagogue schools were present: Judy Perlman for the Sunday School, Joseph Young for the Hebrew School, and Scotty Fohrman for the Nursery School.

After construction of the new community center began, it became apparent that the original design of the structure, which included an auditorium with a lower-level auxiliary hall, would result in a cost of approximately $600,000, far beyond the means of the congregation. For the next several months, revisions to the plans engendered much debate. Finally, in May, 1956, the Board of Directors approved the Building Commission's final plans for a community hall to seat 1,100, an auxiliary hall to seat 250, and a sanctuary to seat 360, as well as a corridor and building connection to the Price mansion.[51] However, fundraising had not kept pace with even the reduced costs of the project and soon funds ran out. Construction was halted in the summer of 1956 and the congregation turned to Eli Field. Under his leadership the first B. E. (Beth El) Day Campaign was

49   Braun's plan provided for a 380-seat sanctuary with a moveable pulpit at its eastern wall that could be moved on steel tracks to the east wall of the adjacent auditorium (or the "community center") for High Holiday services. This concept was abandoned in the sanctuary design of Percival Goodman, adopted in 1961, which had the pulpit located, untraditionally, on the west side of the sanctuary.

50   A special meeting of the Board was held on November 20, 1955, shortly before the groundbreaking ceremony, to approve a $103,000 construction contract for the first phase of the community center and to resolve the protocol for the upcoming groundbreaking ceremony. It was determined that Harold Blumberg would shovel the first spadeful, Allen Gellman would shovel the second spadeful and Edward Glazier would have the third spadeful.

51   The built-in Aeolian pipe organ in the Price mansion was located at the top of the main stairway in the second-floor foyer where a storage closet for items in the Reisman Family Collection is now located. Rabbi Lipis suggested that the organ may be valuable and should be incorporated into the new building's design. This was never done.

held. At its conclusion, an additional $68,000 in pledges was obtained and by August construction on the auditorium building resumed. Sisterhood, always available to assist the congregation, raised funds on its own to equip the modern kitchen.

Construction was not the only eventful occurrence of 1956. In January, the Ritual Committee duly reported that its membership "was graced with the presence of the only woman on the Ritual Committee, Mrs. Morris Futorian." Naomi Futorian was more than just the first woman on Beth El's Ritual Committee. An ardent and accomplished Hebraist and educator, she was an early proponent of a greater role for women in Jewish ritual and an active supporter of intensive Hebrew and Jewish education, both formal and informal.[52] The Ritual Committee also instituted several innovations: the "minyanairs," the regular attendees at the daily *minyan*, would be honored at an annual brunch. (The first honorees were Ben Maccabee,[53] Leo Ginsberg and Sol Shapiro.) The committee also recommended occasionally dedicating Friday night services to a special theme, such as College Night or Family Night; it encouraged Cantor Cohen to participate as a soloist that spring with the Halevi Choir of Chicago; and it endorsed Rabbi Lipis' suggestion of sending Hanukkah parcels, including appropriate reading materials, to children of Beth El members who were attending college.

The Youth Commission that year instituted an important activity which drew many high school students to Beth El: ev-

---

[52] On Saturday morning, December 17, 1949, at Anshe Emet Synagogue in Chicago, Naomi Futorian became the first woman to have an *aliyah* to the Torah at a Conservative synagogue in Chicago. She was also an early and active supporter of Camp Ramah. Later on she was one of the first women chosen by a Beth El nominating committee to serve as a member of the Board of Directors and subsequently was elected as a life-time member of Beth El's Board of Trustees. She passed away in 2002 at the age of 90. In 2017, a main corridor in the Beth El school building was dedicated in her memory by her daughters.

[53] Ben Maccabee was one of the more colorful members of the Beth El family. Soon after joining the congregation, he suggested building a rifle range in the basement of the mansion building in order to teach members of the Men's Club to defend the synagogue against another possible Holocaust. Rabbi Lipis refused to permit it. However, for years afterward during Hanukkah he would display a dagger at morning services in the Sager Bet HaMidrash in remembrance of the might of the Maccabees of old.

ery Sunday night was "Beth El Teen Canteen" at the synagogue. It also instituted the Youth Leadership Award which would be given annually to outstanding young leaders in Beth El's youth groups.

The growth of Beth El's membership, school activities and youth programs, as well as its construction projects and all the other activities taking place at the synagogue created an urgent need for overall supervision of its facilities and its finances. In short, the synagogue needed an executive director. At that time, the office functions were being handled by Miss Mary Giesen, the office secretary, with significant help from the officers and other lay volunteers, but more professional assistance was needed. Although funds were still desperately tight, the Executive Committee in February, 1956 decided (by a vote of four to two) to seek an individual to serve as executive director. That spring, the Board hired Bernard N. Klein, a member of the congregation, to serve as Beth El's first Executive Director.

Early in 1956, the congregation honored Rabbi Lipis on the occasion of his 25th anniversary in the rabbinate. In the spring, the rabbi appeared on television for the first time on the WTTW Channel 11 program *Time For Religion*. The following November, the congregation granted him a leave of absence to serve as Retreat Master in Japan for all Jewish chaplains in the Armed Forces stationed in the Far East.[54] But the fall of 1956 also saw personal tragedy befall the Lipis family when a fire in their home on Lincoln Avenue South took the life of their longtime housekeeper, Mrs. Gertrude Johnson.

Although President Glazier was eager to see the completion of the construction of the new auditorium building, he also displayed a great concern for the educational aspects of the congregation. In September, 1956, building on its already well-established reputation for emphasizing education, the Board of Directors authorized $1,000 for adult education. Until that time, educational and cultural programs for adults had

---

[54] Throughout his tenure at Beth El, Rabbi Lipis maintained an active role in the U.S. Navy Reserve. During the summer of 1955, he had been appointed chaplain of the famous battleship USS New Jersey, the first time a Jewish chaplain had been accorded that honor and responsibility.

been undertaken primarily by volunteers in the congregation or as part of a wider community program, all of which had to be financially self-sustaining. That fall, Irving Kaplan was hired as Youth Director, a position he would hold for several years serving as an inspired leader and mentor for hundreds of Beth El teenagers.[55] Also that September, the Board of Directors was faced with a dilemma: should Beth El participate in the Israel Bond function being held at North Shore Congregation Israel? After considerable debate, it decided to do what many boards often do – it referred the matter to a sub-committee.[56]

By November, 1956, Bernard Klein announced he would be leaving the position of Executive Director and a search was started for his replacement. In the meantime, the office secretary, Mrs. Sonia Lees, was asked to handle his duties, an assignment she undertook in a very "commendable" fashion until she, too, left the synagogue the following June. At the annual meeting in December, in addition to the installation of officers and new directors, Benjamin and Gertrude Harris, who just a short ten years earlier had led a few families in organizing a congregation whose membership had now reached 514 families, presented "their" congregation with a new Torah scroll. It was a moment of great joy for the congregation and immense pride for the Harris family.

1957 began with a renewed focus on the construction of the community center building. Although construction was only four weeks behind schedule, so were the funds to pay the builder. In addition, the greenhouse located on the south side of the coach house needed to be removed to create a new access for traffic onto the property, a cost which had not been included in the original construction budget. That spring, the Board was also faced with the decision of whether to rent or purchase folding chairs for the new auditorium. It decided to buy 1,000 chairs

---

55   Kaplan also appeared as Tiny Tov in the weekly children's television program *The Magic Door*, produced by the Chicago Board of Rabbis.

56   The event, held on November 10, 1956 amidst the international furor surrounding Israel's Suez Campaign in Egypt, featured Mrs. Eleanor Roosevelt as the guest speaker and was well attended by Beth El members.

at $13.50 each, another additional expense. These immediate needs were met, once again, in large part by the efforts of Harold Blumberg. He was able to arrange for a $170,000 mortgage loan from the Oak Park Bank, which was approved on March 7. Soon a letter went out to all congregants declaring: "An emergency exists: we must have cash to pay the contractors." Major efforts were made to collect funds.[57] A motion to raise annual dues to $150 was defeated, but school tuition was raised from $90 to $100 per child. In an effort to control expenses, the Board requested Charlie Albert to supervise the financial accounting for the Building Fund and it changed the congregation's fiscal year so that it ended on June 30 of each year.[58] But the delay in construction did not deter President Glazier. Early in 1957, before the new building had any heat and with gaps in the walls covered with large canvas tarpaulins, the Glazier family invited the congregation into the new community center for their son's bar mitzvah. It was a particularly cold Saturday morning and although a few portable heaters had been brought into the unfinished shell of the structure, the congregation sat huddled in hats, gloves and overcoats while Rabbi Lipis quickly led the regular *Shabbat* morning service for the first time in the new auditorium.

In March, at Rabbi Lipis' urging, the synagogue formally recognized the importance of Jewish summer camping, particularly Camp Ramah, which had been established in Conover, Wisconsin in 1947. The rabbi noted that Beth El already had eighteen young people enrolled for the 1957 summer and the Board approved the motion of Maurice Spertus to establish a

---

57 In January, 1957, the Board also approved a $10 annual director fee to help pay the cost of the annual director's dinner. The fee continued to be collected long after the dinner was discontinued. That March, several directors objected to "the great number of mail matters" sent out from the congregation and suggested a limitation on the number of mailings in order to reduce costs.

58 As part of the efforts to raise funds, the congregation offered dedication opportunities for the new auditorium facilities, except for the kitchen which was officially designated as the "Sisterhood Kitchen."

special fund for scholarships to Jewish summer camps.[59] The rabbi's commitment to developing Jewish leaders for the future was also evident the following month, when *Shabbat* morning services on April 20 were conducted entirely by members of the Tephilin Club.[60]

The spring of 1957 also saw a major change in the educational leadership at the synagogue. Harry Hershman became the Director of Activities, responsible for all arrangements for bar and bat mitzvah celebrations at the synagogue, a position he would hold until his departure from Beth El the following spring. During this period Rabbi Lipis undertook to serve as temporary head of Hebrew education with the important assistance of Naomi Futorian, and on more than one occasion he reported to the Board on the "superb services being provided by Mrs. Futorian" to the Beth El schools. This temporary arrangement would continue until March 13, 1958, when Dr. Louis Katzoff, a respected leader in the field of Jewish education, was hired by the School Board (then under the chairmanship of Bernard Sokol) as the new educational director for the synagogue. Dr. Katzoff was also a rabbi, having been ordained by the Jewish Theological Seminary in 1934. He had received his doctorate at the University of Pennsylvania in 1948[61] and had more recently served as Registrar of the College of Jewish Studies in Chicago (later to be known as the Spertus Institute).

The fall of 1957 saw a flurry of activity as the various synagogue committees rushed to prepare for the first High Holiday services in their own home. As usual, Harold Blumberg was at the forefront, discussing parking arrangements with the High-

---

[59] It was during this period that Rabbi Lipis was instrumental in having Highland Park High School change the night of its graduation ceremonies from Friday to Thursday. He also refused to refer to the public schools' December vacation as "Christmas Vacation," instead calling it the "Mid-Winter Recess."

[60] Participants in this event included Larry Bloom, Daniel Weinberg, Daniel Braver, Joseph Steinberg, Steve Gumbiner and Gershon Ratner.

[61] Dr. Katzoff's first rabbinic position was as the "campus rabbi" at the University of Pennsylvania in 1934, a position newly created by the Philadelphia branch of United Synagogue.

land Park police and heading the group which would obtain the money to purchase the new *aron kodesh* for the services. Of course, he had not given up collecting the funds still needed to pay for the construction. At a special joint meeting of the Board of Directors and the Board of Trustees held on September 29, 1957, it was Harold Blumberg who made the suggestion to declare October 13, 1957 "Pay Your Pledge Week." This was one of the many innovative suggestions which saw Beth El through the financial crisis of the time. Finally, on November 23, 1957, a combined 10th Anniversary Celebration and dedication of the new building was held under the chairmanship of James Lawrence. *Shabbat* and Festival services thereafter were held in the auditorium until the construction of the main sanctuary was completed.

That fall also saw the adoption of new by-laws by the Board of Directors. They had been drafted by Sherman Corwin over a period of many months, and they still form the basis for the current by-laws of the congregation. Also, in November, a new policy was approved by the Board: henceforth, no bar or bat mitzvah would be permitted unless the family's financial obligations to the synagogue had been paid in full. In addition, Mrs. Gertrude Resnick was hired to serve as Beth El's office manager. She proved exceedingly adept at her duties and was soon invited to attend all meetings of the Board of Directors. She provided invaluable services to the congregation for the next three years.[62]

Albert Dolin assumed the presidency of the synagogue at the December, 1957 annual meeting and with it all the "growing pains" of a rapidly increasing population in Highland Park and surrounding communities.[63] With the completion of construction of its large new building, the congregation's agenda was

---

[62]   Mrs. Resnick left Beth El in 1963 to work for Mayer Stiebel's catering organization in Evanston.

[63]   One of Dolin's first "crises" came in March, 1958, when the Sisterhood accused Bernard Kaplan, Vice President of Administration, of charging them for the use of the premises! Kaplan denied this, explaining that he had imposed a fee only for clean-up help. Dolin handled this problem very diplomatically and traditionally – he appointed a committee to look into the matter.

focused, again, on collecting the funds to pay the bills and settling into its new quarters.[64] Eli Field was appointed to head a group of men that would seek collection of unpaid pledges. Although faced with a year-end operating deficit of $20,000 and an anticipated deficit of $60,000 in the next fiscal year, the Board, in June, 1958, again resisted an increase in dues. Instead, Dolin appointed a Special Finance Committee, which included Fred Fell and Leonard Sarnat, that recommended a voluntary pro rata assessment of each member in the amount of $20.87. It was the start of deficit billing which would continue almost annually for the next decade.

Despite all the financial adversity, discussions continued throughout the year about the need to proceed with the final aspect of the original plan for Beth El's expansion: a new sanctuary. However, Isadore Braun's original design for the sanctuary came under criticism. Almost immediately after the auditorium had been completed, complaints were voiced about its poor acoustical qualities and concerns were expressed as to whether this would also be a problem in the sanctuary. In addition, many expressed the desire for a more aesthetically and spiritually satisfying design than the one previously approved. In November, 1958, the Board gave formal approval to a new Sanctuary Campaign with a goal of $400,000 but also directed a search for a new architect to design this most important structure. In May, 1959, the Board authorized President Dolin to negotiate with noted architect Percival Goodman for services in connection with the design and construction of the new sanctuary.

The spring of 1959 saw Beth El actively involved in supporting Israel Bonds and on April 9 the Honorable Abba Eban, Israel's ambassador to the United Nations and the United States, came to Beth El to speak on behalf of that worthwhile cause. But once again the financial condition of the congregation was an issue.

---

64 The designation of memorial opportunities was an important part of the fundraising effort. One of the first items to be dedicated in the new auditorium was the Kahn Stage, given by Mr. and Mrs. Saul Kahn in memory of Irving S. Kahn. Although the stage was removed in the 2013 restoration of the Blumberg Auditorium, the plaque commemorating the Kahn's gift was retained.

As a cost-saving move, the School Board sold the school busses that Beth El had owned and operated for years and contracted with an outside bus company to provide bus service for its school children. And even though dues were increased, these measures proved inadequate to pay off current debts. In June, the congregation borrowed $75,000 from the Continental Illinois National Bank in Chicago. At the same time the congregation's leadership forged ahead with the plans to build the sanctuary. In May, 1959, Martin E. Janis, a professional fundraiser, was hired to direct the Sanctuary Campaign. That same month the Board made an historic decision which would affect the quality of Jewish education at Beth El for many years into the future. It courageously adopted the "radical" recommendation of Dr. Katzoff, strongly supported by the School Board, to eliminate over a period of a few years all English language Sunday School classes and to require Hebrew education for all children between the ages of nine and thirteen. Up to that point, the enrollment of the Hebrew School was comprised primarily of boys, with girls generally attending the Sunday School. In urging this change in educational policy, Dr. Katzoff strongly encouraged "minimum standards for all of our children" and emphasized the importance of having girls as well as boys involved in Hebrew education. He asserted his belief that it was "incumbent to equip all our students, and especially the girls, to lead useful lives of understanding Jews...." Wrote Dr. Katzoff in his report to the Board: "When you educate a boy, you educate an individual. When you educate a girl, you educate a family."

By the summer of 1959, Beth El's member families numbered 678.[65] This increase in membership already had outgrown the capacity of the new auditorium and Bennett Shulman, Vice President Ritual, investigated the possibility of using the Highland

---

65   At the August 6, 1959 Board of Directors meeting, Leonard Braver served as acting secretary. He noted that a proposal made to limit membership in the congregation was deferred "in order to create new and additional headaches for another meeting." But this sizeable membership soon resulted in the creation of several new committees: Committee on Adjustments (for members who could not afford the dues), Gifts to the Synagogue Committee (to determine what gifts from members were appropriate), and a Long Range Membership Policies Committee!

Park High School auditorium for additional High Holiday services that fall.[66] The increased demand to use the new kitchen and auditorium for social functions led to lengthy discussions on the catering situation and in December, 1959 the Board approved the motion of Eli Field to appoint Mayer Stiebel as Beth El's first official caterer, a position he would occupy for four years. Also that year, Bernard Gately was hired as the "houseman," or chief custodian, and he moved into the apartment above the kitchen in the auditorium building.

Edward Glazier and Harold Blumberg assumed joint chairmanship of the General Campaign for construction of the sanctuary in 1959 and by December of that year Leonard Birnbaum reported pledges had risen to $216,000. As the directors moved closer to actual construction, they remembered the problems encountered when the auditorium project had begun without adequate resources. This time they were determined to avoid those problems. They carefully budgeted the sources of funds for the project. In September, 1960, the Board, still short of adequate pledges but determined to build a sanctuary for the entire congregation, adopted a resolution that "a minimum participating assessment [of $300] be made on each member of the Congregation to contribute to the Sanctuary Building Fund Campaign commencing with the year 1960, with the appropriate committee having authority to arrange greater flexibility in time of payment where hardship exists." The following year, this concept was expanded to cover each new member, so that all members would have an obligation to help pay for the synagogue's expanded physical facilities. This was the beginning of the Building Fund assessment for new members.

1960 also saw significant developments in other areas of the congregation which would have long-range implications. In March, Mel Stark, a farsighted member of the School Board, made an impressive presentation to the Board of Directors on the School Board's concept of Jewish education at Beth El, stat-

---

66   That fall, Dr. Katzoff had graciously served on the pulpit at Shaare Tikvah Synagogue in Chicago during the High Holidays due to the illness of its rabbi, Morris A. Gutstein.

ing that the "education of a child is not only the responsibility of its parents, but also of the entire community. Thus, the schools should not be expected to be [financially] self-sustaining." This became the basis for all future educational policies at the synagogue. The following September, Beth El joined with North Shore Congregation Israel and Temple B'nai Torah in encouraging the College of Jewish Studies, then located at 72 East 11th Street in Chicago, to open a North Shore branch for both youth and adult studies. Soon, Beth El had the highest enrollment in this new educational endeavor.

Throughout the 1950s, Sisterhood had been a key participant in providing important programs and involving many women in the life of the congregation. One of its most popular activities was the annual Selling Bee, which drew hundreds of people to shop for quality merchandise which had been donated to the organization.[67] During the summer of 1960, Pearl White announced Sisterhood's decision to end its annual Selling Bee and instead hold a Festival of the Arts and Crafts on the weekend of November 12 and 13. It was a huge success and the Art Festival continued annually thereafter for many years.[68] In fact, however, Sisterhood did not end its Selling Bee that year. It continued to be held successfully for several more years.

In October, 1960, the Board amended its by-laws so that the recording secretary would not be subject to a three-year limit in office. This was done specifically to permit Sherman Corwin, who had done a superb job in keeping the minutes and overseeing legal matters for the congregation since 1958, to remain in that position. He would continue to serve the congregation as recording secretary until June, 1966. At the same meeting, Rabbi Lipis urged participation by all officers, directors and trustees in the congregation's religious services and suggested that this be made a condition of Board membership. This idea was soon incorporated into the synagogue's by-laws.

---

[67] At the Selling Bee held in March, 1959 at the Highland Park Recreation Center, the famous comedian Jerry Lewis was the guest attraction. The place was packed!

[68] The 2nd Annual Art Festival was held over the weekend of November 4-5, 1961. The cost of admission for the entire weekend was $1.00.

On December 11, 1960, Rabbi and Shoshanah Lipis were honored at a dinner celebrating their tenth anniversary at Beth El: ten years of dedication and devotion to the spiritual needs of the Beth El family, of turning dreams into realities. Shortly thereafter, Eli Field became president of Beth El. Although he gathered about him many of the same enthusiastic men and women who had worked through the years to create new facilities, he also introduced many innovations. Field wasn't joking when he wrote to the directors in May, 1961: "Things are happening at Beth El and there is lots to be done!"

One of the first innovations was to hold an all-day seminar for the Executive Committee, presidents of all auxiliaries, and the professional staff at the Illinois Beach State Park in Zion on January 22, 1961. In February, after many years of encouragement by the rabbi, the Board gave approval to a plan negotiated by Bennett Shulman with Shalom Memorial Park in Arlington Heights to create a permanent Beth El Section at that cemetery. Also, the Board approved changing the date of the congregation's annual meeting to May or June of each year to allow each new administration time to organize and develop plans over the summer months before the beginning of a new year of activities.

But still at the forefront of the synagogue's agenda was its dream of a new sanctuary. The Board had approved the design of Percival Goodman for the sanctuary, a "jeweled crown" with colored windows dominating and complementing the existing facilities. Harry Rubin was appointed to arrange the groundbreaking ceremonies for the sanctuary, scheduled for June 11, 1961. It was a noteworthy event, attended by many dignitaries including United States Senator Everett M. Dirksen, Congresswoman Margaret Stitt Church, and Mayor Robert Cushman of Highland Park. Shortly thereafter, to assure adequate funds for the building project, and with close to $500,000 in pledges already in hand, the congregation approved a $350,000 mortgage loan from the Continental Illinois National Bank, part of which was used to repay the existing loan. With what seemed like a sound financial plan in place, the Board entered into a construction contract with Harvey Hanson & Co, General Contractor, to build the sanctuary for a cost not to exceed $515,000. In light of the relatively balanced fiscal situation, no appeal for funds was scheduled for *Kol Nidre* that fall, a decision which would be dramatically reversed the following year.

In the midst of this important undertaking, other events of special significance continued to enhance the synagogue. On October 1, 1961, three Torah scrolls were dedicated and presented to the synagogue by Rabbi Philip and Shoshanah Lipis, Joseph and Ethel Horwitz, and Bernard and Rochelle Zell in honor of their respective twenty-fifth wedding anniversaries. Also in October, the Adult Jewish Studies Program began its year with a visit by Mrs. Eleanor Roosevelt, who earlier in the evening had been the guest of honor for dinner at the home of Joseph and Mae Gray. In December, the Board of Directors accepted the monumental offer of Maurice and Badona Spertus to establish at Beth El an Institute of Judaica and a Museum of Judaic ritual, historical, and contemporary art "to elevate the cultural standards of the Jewish people" and to promote understanding with the community's non-Jewish neighbors. As a result of this action, the Kol Ami (Voice of My People) Museum was established at Beth El, funded initially with several important gifts from the Spertus' private collection. However, the scope of the original plan of Spertus proved too great for the synagogue. Although a nine-member Board of Governors for the proposed Spertus Institute of Judaica was elected by the Board of Directors (which included Maurice Spertus, Herman Spertus, Benjamin Harris, Bernard Sokol, Harold Blumberg and Adina Katzoff, the highly talented wife of Dr. Louis Katzoff), the Spertus Institute never took hold at the synagogue.[69] Beth El did not have the resources, facilities, faculty or commitment to sustain what Mr. and Mrs. Spertus intended would be a scholarly institution.[70]

---

[69] A scholarly compilation entitled "*Mah nishtana*, A Selection of One Hundred and Eleven Passover Hagadot," authored by Harry I. Hirschhorn with assistance from Mrs. Katzoff, was published in 1964 in conjunction with a major exhibition at the Kol Ami Museum.

[70] A few years later, the Spertus family generously endowed the College of Jewish Studies in Chicago, which eventually became the Spertus Institute of Jewish Studies, a leading institution for Jewish education.

By the fall of 1961, membership in the congregation had risen to 702 families and annual dues had increased to $200. School enrollment [71] had soared to 852 children ranging from kindergarten through Hebrew High School,[72] with many Hebrew School students participating in the innovative Hebrew Skills Program on *Shabbat* mornings instituted by Dr. Katzoff, which taught familiarity with prayers in the *siddur*. Milt Leeds reported that over 300 young people were being served by the Youth Commission, the largest group being USY (United Synagogue Youth), but also a significant contingent of high school youth was active in LTF (Leaders Training Fellowship), led by its own youth advisor and teacher, Michael Newberger. The Tephilin Club, for boys in 7th and 8th grades, sponsored a weekly Sunday breakfast following *minyan* and also a popular bowling league. Its longtime club advisors were Joseph Gray and Harry Young, both members of the Men's Club. In July, 1962, two of its members, Brian Braun and Howard Lipschultz, published *Flashbacks*, a history of the Tephilin Club since its founding in 1948.[73]

In the winter of 1962, the congregation sponsored an outstanding fundraising event: Arnold Shure and then Ben Sager chaired a committee which included all three auxiliaries to present a concert at the Highland Park High School auditorium featuring the renowned cantor and soloist, the "world's greatest tenor," Richard Tucker. The event was publicized on the cover of the February 8 issue of the *Highland Park News*. That spring, the Board, at the suggestion of Bernard Sokol, recommended once again employing an executive director whose

---

71 During the early 1960s, the school organized an annual spring faculty-student softball game at the Ravinia School playground. Dr. Katzoff played second base, Cantor Cohen played first base, and Rabbi Lipis was an outstanding shortstop.

72 The Hebrew High School held its first graduation exercises on June 22, 1962. The class consisted of nine students: Diane Albert, David Benson, Arthur Rosby, Anita Spertus, Miriam ("Mop") Steinberg, Morton Steinberg, Robert Sternberg, Jerry Taxy and Marc Young. Their pictures were featured on the cover of the *Highland Park News*.

73 Many of the Tephilin Club's early presidents included individuals who would later become prominent in the Chicago community, including Avrum Gray (1948-1950), Sheldon Gray (1952-1953), Larry Field (1953-1954), Sam Zell (1955-1956), and Larry Bloom (1957-1958).

functions initially would be to assist in the area of fundraising for the new sanctuary. In May, 1962, David Weinstein was hired for that position. Later that year, from December 23 to 27, the Beth El LTF group, led by Jerry Taxy, hosted over 100 high school students from different Midwestern cities for the 16th Annual Midwest LTF Kallah (convention).

As construction of the new sanctuary progressed during 1962, it soon became apparent that the careful plans for the payment of the project were not being fulfilled, primarily because congregants were not paying their pledges; once again a cash crisis existed. In addition, numerous items not included in the original construction contract, but essential to the project, were authorized: the garage building, part of the original Price Estate, had to be demolished and cleared away; a new parking lot and driveways needed to be graded and paved and provided with adequate drainage; and large, movable doors separating the sanctuary from the new reception lounge (later the Paset Lounge) needed to be ordered. Quickly, steps were taken to solve the problem. Harold Blumberg, still at the forefront of Beth El's leadership, held a series of parlor meetings with the trustees and others to raise cash. President Field appointed a committee of founders "to consult with" members who had not participated in the Building Fund at the time they requested High Holiday seating assignments. Directors made phone calls to individuals who were behind in their pledges. Finally, the following spring, after the general contractor threatened legal action, teams of two directors each under the direction of Jack Solovy spent Sunday, March 24, 1963 going from house to house making personal solicitations to collect unpaid pledges. All these efforts paid off and eventually satisfactory arrangements were made to pay all debts.

Under the direction of Irving Finkle, chairman of the Building Commission, construction proceeded on schedule and the new sanctuary was available for the 1962 High Holiday services. It was a grand occasion. Jerome Sternberg had been responsible for preparing the newly constructed but unfurnished building for the High Holidays and he, together with building housekeepers

Paul and Sylvia Havel, did an outstanding job. At services that fall Rabbi Lipis, standing on the uppermost level of the new *bimah*, looked out over a gathering of almost 1,800 individuals, beaming with pride at the accomplishments the congregation had achieved over the past eleven years. But funds were still desperately needed and on *Kol Nidre* evening that Yom Kippur the leadership of the congregation once again conducted an intensive "old fashioned" appeal, announcing the names of those who came forward and the amount of each pledge. It was a long evening and the following month Rabbi Lipis urged the elimination of an appeal on Yom Kippur.

Another innovation of President Field was to focus meetings of directors on specific topics so in-depth reports and discussions could be held. In the fall of 1962, one such meeting dealt with Beth El's membership, which seemed to have leveled off and was not growing. Many reasons were attributed as the cause of this problem, none authoritative, but suggestions were made to try and resolve this phenomenon. As a result, within a few months a Golden Age Group was created and soon a Young Couples Club was founded and held its first open meeting at the synagogue under co-chairmen Ernest Kaplan and Gerald Buckman. It would soon be known as the Couples Club and it became an active auxiliary at the congregation. Also, the Lipises began to hold regular "Coffee and ... with the Rabbi" meetings in their home on Sunday evenings to meet and greet new members of the congregation. At another in-depth Board meeting, in January, 1963, the Youth Commission reported on its important role in the congregation: Jerry Taxy, president of LTF, and Brian Marcus, president of USY, presented reports to the directors. Jack Shapiro, Vice President Education, also noted that Beth El by then had the largest Jewish nursery school in the entire Chicago area.

In the spring of 1963, the congregation gathered in the auditorium to honor and celebrate with Jordan and Marcia Cohen on the occasion of their tenth anniversary with Beth El. Then on May 10, at Friday night *Shabbat* services, the congregation gathered for a special "Yom Moreh" ("Teacher's Day") to honor Dr. Louis

Katzoff on the occasion of his fifth anniversary as educational director at the synagogue.[74] Notable changes in personnel also occurred that year. In June, Bernard Sokol became congregational president.[75] Irving Kaplan, youth director for seven years, left Beth El, eventually to make *aliyah* to Israel. Cyril Oldham was hired as executive director and would serve the congregation ably for the next eight years. Ray Havelock became the new chief custodian for the expanded facilities. Also, for the first time, discussions were held on the need to hire a "sexton" to assist in the many religious functions at the congregation, a suggestion which would be implemented a few years later. That year the Sisterhood, at the urging of Shoshanah Lipis and Jo Sternberg, instituted a new program: Torah Fund classes, which were not only enlightening to its participants but also helped fund the Mathilda Schechter student dormitory at the Jewish Theological Seminary in New York.[76]

The summer of 1963 saw Beth El's membership becoming involved in events taking place on a national scale. The civil rights movement, begun in the late 1950s and early 1960s, embodied the traditional Jewish feeling for freedom and justice for all peoples. The Men's Club had formed a Social Action Committee, intending to alert its members to issues of social significance. In August, that group proposed that the congregation's Board of Directors adopt a resolution supporting President John F. Kennedy's civil rights program. It did and the congregation sent a telegram to the White House expressing this support. The following month, the Board approved another recommendation of the Men's Club Social Action Committee, this one in support of "open housing" and calling for "the passage of such legislation

74   For the High Holidays in 1963, Dr. Katzoff engaged Tom Lanyi, an alum of the Beth El Hebrew School, to serve as coordinator of three separate youth services. Among the student service leaders were Charles Feinberg, Leah Zell, Jerry Taxy, Mona DeKoven, Naomi Boxerman, Karen Robbin, Amy Goldman and Robert Sternberg.

75   Bernard Sokol tragically lost his life in an automobile accident in Highland Park in 1969. Soon afterward, the Bernard H. Sokol Youth and Education Foundation was established at Beth El.

76   The Mathilda Schechter dormitory was sold by the Seminary in 2016 to raise needed funds for a new construction project.

as will truly make a land of the free, for our nation, with one law for all Americans, regardless of race, color, creed, or national origin." These actions created such interest that suggestions were made for the congregation to establish its own social action committee (something that finally occurred in 1968, with Ruth Belzer as its chair). Suddenly, the congregation was overcome with shock and grief when President Kennedy was assassinated on November 22, 1963. Two days later the congregation gathered in its new sanctuary for a special memorial service for the slain young president. In his memory, a donation was made by the congregation to the Kennedy Foundation for Retarded Children, a favorite Kennedy charity, and at the suggestion of Benjamin Harris, a permanent bronze memorial plaque was affixed to the wall in the lobby of the sanctuary.[77]

Although the new sanctuary had been constructed, the interior had not been completely finished. In the summer of 1963, the Board approved a loan of $500,000 to refinance the existing debt and also to permit the installation of air conditioning, permanent seats, carpeting and pulpit furniture.[78] That fall, in response to Rabbi Lipis' concerns, a new format for the *Kol Nidre* appeal was introduced: a card with fold-down tabs was distributed, so gifts could be made and recorded in a "dignified manner" following a short address from the pulpit. This "silent appeal" continues to the present.

In 1964,[79] under the direction of Jack Solovy, a new type of fundraising activity was attempted and proved to be an overwhelming success. "Jubilee 64" was a grand extravaganza held at the Arie Crown Theater in the old McCormick Place in

---

[77] This plaque was relocated to the central corridor opposite the Sisterhood gift shop in 2000 and subsequently placed adjacent to the entrance to the Gray Cultural and Learning Center in 2017.

[78] By the following June, for the first time in many years, the Board approved a balanced budget, thus eliminating the need for deficit billings.

[79] In May, 1964, the directors passed a resolution extending "their congratulations to Mrs. Sternberg on her installation as Sisterhood President." Josephine Sternberg would serve the congregation in various capacities continuously and with great distinction for the next quarter of a century.

Chicago with Irv Kupcinet serving as emcee and featuring comedian Sam Levenson and other entertainers. (It was so successful that the Board quickly authorized reserving the Civic Theatre in Chicago for "Jubilee 65," which featured a performance by popular comedian Shelly Berman.) Soon afterward, the magnificent gates for the Kol Ami Museum, created in Israel by artist Henri (Nechemiah) Azaz, arrived and were installed in time for the first public display in the museum.[80] In the fall of 1964, Dr. Sheldon Kamin, Youth Vice President, announced that Larry Stern would be serving as the new youth director.[81]

The culmination of years of dreaming and hard work was reached over the weekend of November 27 and 28, 1964 when the new sanctuary was formally dedicated at services and celebrations organized by Eli Field.[82] Among those addressing the congregation on that momentous occasion were Dr. Max Arzt, Vice-Chancellor of the Jewish Theological Seminary, Rabbi Ben Zion Kaganoff, president of the Chicago Board of Rabbis, Fred Gieser, mayor of Highland Park, and Gail Sokol, president of the Beth El Youth Group. Emphasizing the importance of education and the role of the youth in the congregation, the *Shabbat* morning services were led entirely by students of Beth El's schools, including David Eisenberg, Leah Zell, Ronnie Sokol, Harold Benson, Mitchell Taxy, Karen Robbin, Laurel Bucky and David Sager. A *"minyan"* of cantors, including Beth El's own Jordan Cohen, presented a special concert to honor the new house of worship.

Soon, a flurry of special events and dedications occurred. In January, 1965, the first annual Ronald and Ethel Taub Lecture was

---

80   The gates were removed in 2016 during the renovation of the corridor surrounding the Field Family Sanctuary.

81   That December, the Men's Club, under Chairman Daniel Tauman, presented another of its successful productions, "My Fair Maidel" starring Albert Gorchoff, Len Birnbaum, Lovey Durschlag, Joan Bernick and Mort Taxy, as part of its annual Candle Light Supper Dance. The following year, under Chairman Sidney Attenberg, it produced another successful production: "Shalom Solly, or There's No Business Like Schul Business."

82   The cover of the November 26, 1964 edition of the *Highland Park News* featured a photograph of the new sanctuary with Rabbi Lipis, Bernard Sokol and Eli Field standing before the open ark containing all ten *sifrei* Torah of the congregation.

held at the synagogue: the featured speaker was Dr. Will Herberg and it was an overwhelming success. In the spring of 1965, the new reception area adjacent to the sanctuary was dedicated as the Paset Lounge in honor of Nathan and Rose Paset. Later that year a magnificent tapestry which adorns the south wall of the Paset Lounge was donated to the congregation by Mr. and Mrs. Maurice Spertus. It had been found in Europe, cut into four sections and used as a runner; when pieced back together, the tapestry depicted an interior view of King Solomon's Temple by an unknown artisan. That summer, the Sisterhood, once again displaying its continued support for the congregation, donated $10,000 for the honor of having the doors of the ark dedicated in honor of that vital organization.

By the summer of 1965, when Max Applebaum became Beth El's seventh president, Hy London, Membership Vice President, announced that the congregation had 779 member families, and Harold Gorin, Financial Vice President, was able to advise the congregation that all its current debts had been paid and $100,000 was in the bank!

Rabbi Lipis' continued role as a chaplain in the U.S. Navy Reserve eventually led to his attaining the rank of commander. In January, 1966, he was called upon by the Department of Defense to serve as Retreat Master for all Jewish chaplains serving in Europe. Having been granted the temporary rank of general in the United States Army, General Lipis, accompanied by Shoshanah, visited the Dachau concentration camp and later led a group of sixty-five Jewish chaplains in the study of Torah at the retreat's headquarters in Berchtesgaden, Germany, the very site where only a few years earlier the Nazis had plotted the extermination of the Jewish people. This was an extremely emotional occasion for the Rabbi and Shoshanah Lipis and one that brought pride to every member of Beth El. During Rabbi Lipis' absence, the congregation called upon one of its own members, Rabbi Mordecai Simon, Executive Director of the Chicago Board of Rabbis, to fill the rabbinic role at Beth El on an interim basis. This was the first of numerous occasions over the next four decades on which Rabbi Simon would undertake this important function.

In 1966, as an outgrowth of President Lyndon B. Johnson's Head Start Program, Beth El instituted the Summer Urban Gateway day camp program at the synagogue for disadvantaged children. It ran successfully for several summers alongside the regular summer day camp. That same year, Ted Weinstein organized the first Twi-light Golf League for the Men's Club.

The growth of the congregation continued in 1966 and by Rosh Hashanah that fall membership had reached 870 families and Irving Robbin, Education Vice President, reported school enrollment of 1,090 children. At the same time, Sam Rade, Ritual Vice President, announced to the Board that an astounding 110 bar and bat mitzvah celebrations were scheduled for that year. He also formed a committee to limit the elaborateness of the *oneg Shabbat* celebrations which followed many bar and bat mitzvah services. Once again, the Board of Directors appointed a committee to consider a limitation on the size of the congregation, an idea which, once again, did not succeed.

Rabbi Lipis, who had given so much to the congregation since his arrival in 1951, was granted a well-deserved sabbatical in Israel "for study and self-examination" during the first half of 1967. (A gala "bon voyage" *oneg Shabbat* planned for Rabbi and Shoshanah Lipis on the eve of their departure had to be cancelled due to the infamous snowstorm of that January which struck the Chicago area.) On their return, the Lipises were honored guests at the commencement ceremonies of the Jewish Theological Seminary in New York at which the Chancellor, Dr. Louis Finkelstein, bestowed upon Rabbi Lipis the degree of Honorary Doctor of Divinity.

Suddenly, the focus of the congregation was again directed to the world scene as the Six Day War in Israel began on June 5, 1967. Newly installed President Ben Sager called an emergency meeting of the congregation to offer special prayers and express support for Israel. Emergency fundraising was also undertaken to help the Jewish state in its hour of need. That fall, the Israel Bond dinner honoring Rabbi and Mrs. Lipis raised over $150,000.

1967 also brought major new additions to the interior of the synagogue's facilities. A committee headed by Leonard Birnbaum had undertaken the reconstruction of the "old" sanctuary, by then called the "small sanctuary." (Two years later, through the generosity of Ben and Florence Sager, it became known as the Sager Bet HaMidrash.) The work also included the remodeling of the auditorium. But the highlight of the committee's efforts was the beautification of the main sanctuary. The ark doors, interior adornments, *ner tamid* and *menorah*, all designed by world-renowned Jewish designer Ludwig Wolpert, were installed and ready for the High Holiday services that fall. And at a special meeting of the Board of Directors on October 29, the refurnished auditorium was formally declared to be the Harold and Ruby Blumberg Auditorium. For many years Harold had rightfully been called "Mr. Beth El" and at a dedication ceremony the following April, the Blumbergs were honored for their many contributions to the congregation since its earliest days.

Major changes in staff occurred in 1967. Larry Stern left the community and was replaced as youth director by Gerald Kaye. In July, the Board of Directors approved the hiring of Reverend Isaac Kornfeld of Montreal, Canada as "sexton, librarian, curator of the Kol Ami Museum and teacher for bar and bat mitzvah training." Reverend Kornfeld would make a lasting contribution for many years to come.[83] He began by leading the youth services that Rosh Hashanah, which were held for the first time at the Murray Theater at Ravinia Park. Milt Fields had recommended that location to replace the large tent which had been erected on the synagogue grounds for the two previous years.

Couples Club, which had been growing along with the congregation, inaugurated a new program in the fall of 1967 under its president Mel Pollack. It was a progressive visit to the sukkot of various congregants. Initially called the "Sukkie Lookie," the Sukkah Walk would become an annual Beth El tradition. Also that year, the School Board, under the guidance of Irving Robbin, instituted a new Baccalaureate Program designed to replace the Confirmation Class with a more intense education-

---

[83]   Some of Reverend Kornfeld's most interesting achievements included the publication in 1982 of his extensively researched *A History of Meals in Jewish Life*, and in 1990 *The Jewish Women*, in English and Hebrew. In both of these he identified himself as Yitzchak Kornfeld-Degani.

al experience coupled with a financial scholarship for a six-week tour of Israel upon completion of studies. It was a program of which Rabbi Lipis was especially proud. (In 1973, the name of the program was changed to the Israel Scholarship Program.)[84]

The year 1968 started with a shock. In a letter dated January 3, Rabbi Lipis advised President Sager and the Board of Directors of his desire to be relieved of his duties. By now age sixty-two, the rabbi and Shoshanah expressed an interest in spending their "retirement years" in Israel and California, where their two daughters had moved. Although he knew that "the years my family and I have been in Highland Park in association with Beth El, have been among the happiest, most creative, and most fulfilling" of his career in the rabbinate, he felt he had achieved the primary goal he had set for himself when coming to Beth El: to prove the viability of traditional Judaism within the context of modern Americanism. Reluctantly, the Board acceded to his request and by July a separation agreement had been negotiated and approved. Later that month he was designated as Rabbi Emeritus of the congregation. In April of the same year, the country was shaken by the assassination of Dr. Martin Luther King, Jr. and the Board of Directors recognized this tragic loss with appropriate resolutions and expressions of genuine sorrow.

Still, the congregation, its affiliate organizations and school continued its pattern of activity and seemingly endless growth. In March of 1968, in an attempt to upgrade and improve the means of communication between the synagogue and its congregants, Beth El initiated the monthly publication *Impact*, a magazine-styled bulletin printed on heavy glossy paper and containing articles about individual congregants as well as synagogue news. Edited by M.D. "Mush" Oberman, it was well written but costly to produce and its last issue was in July, 1969. In May, 1968, the Beth El LTF group, now led by members Sheryl Robbin and Ellen Gorin, once again hosted a large group of

---

84   1967 was also the year that *The Lakeville Studies; Jewish Identity on the Suburban Frontier* was published by sociologist Marshall Sklare, a critical work based on research done in the Beth El community during the late 1950s, a study in which Rabbi Lipis did not find much, if any, favor.

LTFers from the Chicago area for its annual Spring Seminar.[85] School enrollment in 1969 reached a record of 1,131 students. Space for the school, library and administrative aspects of the congregation was at a premium. Space was so scarce that classes once again were held on *Shabbat* and consideration was once again given to off-site locations and portable classrooms. Ted Bloch, Administrative Vice President, presented a carefully detailed program to construct additional classrooms on the second floor of the mansion building and to add a second story addition to the school building at a cost of approximately $375,000. Although the plan was approved by the Board of Directors in February, 1969, lack of enthusiasm kept it from being implemented.[86]

In the spring of 1969, an "unfortunate, regrettable incident" occurred at the synagogue: Harold Gorin, then Vice President Administration, discovered a few containers of non-kosher food in the synagogue kitchen. The items had been delivered in error by a popular outside kosher caterer. The matter was thoroughly investigated by the Ritual Committee and in a letter to the congregation, President Sager assured all that the "kitchen, its dishes, utensils, and all other equipment...meet the highest standards...of the dietary laws." Nonetheless, the caterer was asked to cease functions at the synagogue after July 6 of that summer.

In more ways than one, 1969 marked the close of a chapter in the history of Beth El. Since 1966, Cantor Cohen had been ill, his condition becoming progressively worse. Often unable to fulfill his role as *shaliach tzibur*, many congregants, most notably Bernard Sokol and Leon Lebow, took over the cantorial functions whenever necessary. In early 1967, Sam Rade, Ritual Vice President, had advised the Board of Directors that the cantor

---

85 Beth El would also host the 1971 LTF Spring Kallah, but by the mid-1970s, the Jewish Theological Seminary had decided to cease supporting this youth organization and it was formally dissolved in 1976.

86 In the spring of 1969, a sewer easement along the Beth El beach was granted to the North Shore Sanitary District. It is probably the only easement owned by that public agency which prohibits construction "on the Jewish High Holidays of Rosh Hashanah and Yom Kipper of any year."

was visiting the Mayo Clinic for a series of examinations which might prove helpful. But his physical condition continued to deteriorate. The High Holidays of 1968 were his last. Although weakened by illness, no one who was present will ever forget the sweetness of Cantor Cohen's voice and the fervency of his prayers as he chanted the liturgy.[87] Finally, the end came on April 21, 1969. He was only forty-two years of age when he died. At his funeral two days later, the congregation filled every corner of the sanctuary as Rabbi Lipis, tears in his voice, eulogized the man who had served Beth El as cantor for sixteen years. "He was our dear, devoted, faithful, utterly selfless friend, yours and mine, teacher of our young, comforter of our bereaved, cheer-bearer to the sick, and the bringer of light to our community." The rabbi looked down at his friend and concluded: "Goodbye Jordan, sweet singer in Israel. We shall miss you. We shall mourn for you. We shall not forget you."

In July, 1969, Rabbi Lipis stepped down as spiritual leader of the congregation he had led for eighteen years. He had guided a small suburban congregation of under 300 families as it grew to become one of the largest and most respected Conservative synagogues in the country. Although not one of the original founders, few would doubt that Philip L. Lipis was the true builder of Beth El. For eighteen years he was the mortar that held the congregation together and the inspiration for undertaking bold new endeavors. He had overseen three separate building campaigns, but he also developed a strong tradition of education and service within the congregation. Utilizing his gift of humor and personal warmth, yet ready always to impose his stern sense of discipline, Rabbi Lipis lavished his attention on programs for the future generations of Conservative Jewry. He encouraged hundreds of children to attend Camp Ramah, he held Talmud classes in his home on *Shabbat* afternoons for teenagers, he was always seeking ways to improve the school, and he was one of the earliest and most effective supporters of the

---

[87] Unbeknown to most, the High Holiday services of 1968 were tape recorded at the behest of Cantor Cohen. These reel-to-reel tapes were donated to the Beth El archives by the cantor's son Alfred in 2017.

Solomon Schechter Day School. So at the farewell testimonial dinner party held at the synagogue on July 13, 1969, it was with much warmth, love and nostalgia that the congregation said goodbye to Philip and Shoshanah Lipis.

"Bonita Vista"

Old World Charm
Combined with
Modern Living

1201 SHERIDAN ROAD
HIGHLAND PARK, ILL.

The 1945 sales brochure for "Bonita Vista," the mansion built by Edward Valentine Price in 1911 at 1201 Sheridan Road in Highland Park, Illinois. Harry Kunin had purchased the property in 1934 from the probate estate of Price for a reported $80,000. He placed the property on the market in 1945 when he retired to California. Mr. and Mrs. Raymond Grunwald purchased it that year for approximately $145,000. (Beth El Archives)

A view of the main entry into the Price mansion beneath the front porte-cochère. This area is now the entrance into Beth El's Gray Cultural and Learning Center. (Beth El Archives)

A view towards Sheridan Road in 1945 of the extensive vegetable garden, the coach house (called the "gardener's cottage" by Mr. Price) and its adjacent greenhouse. This area is now the south portion of the synagogue's parking lot; the current entry into the synagogue grounds is located where the greenhouse once stood. (Beth El Archives)

The sun parlor of the Price mansion, circa 1923. This room became the sanctuary after Beth El purchased the Price Estate in 1948. Today it is the Sager Beit HaMidrash. (Courtesy of the Highland Park Public Library.)

BENJAMIN R. HARRIS

885 ELM PLACE

GLENCOE, ILL.

March 22, 1944

It gives me much pleasure to invite you to a meeting at my home, 885 Elm Place, Glencoe, this Sunday, March 26, at 10:30 A.M., in order to discuss the organization of a Conservative Congregation on the North Shore.

Many of us have been discussing this matter informally for some time. This past Sunday a group met at my home, at which time we discussed the enclosed "Partial Statement of Principles and Program" of the proposed Congregation. This Sunday we will further consider this matter and expect to come to a definite organizational program.

I trust that you will find it possible to be with us at that time, as we are most anxious to have the benefit of your advice and counsel in this matter.

Looking forward to the pleasure of seeing you Sunday at 10:30 A.M. at my home, I remain

Sincerely yours,

Letter from Benjamin Harris sent to several individuals inviting them to a meeting at his home in Glencoe, Illinois on Sunday, March 26, 1944 "to discuss the organization of a Conservative Congregation on the North Shore." This is recognized as the beginning of the process which culminated in the founding of North Suburban Synagogue Beth El. (Beth El Archives)

COUNCIL of CONSERVATIVE SYNAGOGUES of Chicago

203 N. WABASH AVENUE   •   TELEPHONE
CHICAGO 1, ILLINOIS   CENTRAL 8166

February 8, 1945

Dear Dr. Goldman:

   As you undoubtedly know, many of us on the North Shore have been endeavoring to establish a Conservative Congregation in our area. We feel that the time is now ripe for us to make a determined effort to realize that aspiration.

   In view of the tremendous prestige which you enjoy in your community, we feel that your assistance and leadership is essential to us in the realization of this goal. We have been in hopes that we could arrange a meeting which you could address, but were prevented from doing so up to this point due to the difficulty of securing a meeting place. I learned today, however, that it would be possible to use the facilities of the Glencoe Public Library on the nights of Tuesday, March 6, or Thursday, March 8. I am therefore issuing this invitation to you on behalf of the North Shore Committee and trust that despite your very busy schedule you will be able to aid us in furthering our aims.

   I will be out of the city for the next week or two, but if you will be kind enough to inform Rabbi Rabinowitz of your feelings in the matter, I am sure that he can make the necessary arrangements.

   Thanking you for your kind interest, I am

                          Sincerely yours,

                          B. R. Harris

                          Benjamin R. Harris

Dr. Solomon Goldman
Anshe Emet Synagogue
Pine Grove at Grace St.
Chicago, Ill.

Letter dated February 8, 1945 from Benjamin Harris, then an officer of the Council of Conservative Synagogues of Chicago, to Dr. Solomon Goldman, Rabbi of Anshe Emet Synagogue in Chicago, inviting him to meet with the "North Shore Committee" at the Glencoe Public Library to assist in establishing a Conservative congregation "in our area." (American Jewish Archives, Cincinnati, Ohio)

Benjamin and Gertrude Harris in 1956. They initiated the founding of Beth El in 1944. (Photo by Michael Saper; Beth El Archives)

MAY USE HOME ON NORTH SHORE AS A SYNAGOG

BY AL CHASE

Reports that one of Highland Park's residential showplaces, the large stone mansion at 1201 Sheridan rd., will be used as a synagog were partly confirmed yesterday. Max Goldberg, president of the Illinois Baking corporation, who bought the property from Raymond Grunwald, president of the Grunwald Hard Chrome Plating Company, Inc., said a new synagog would not be erected on the property but added that the use of part of the residence as a synagog had been considered.

"I intend to use it not only for my residence but also for a community project or center, for charitable or educational purposes, or for worship," said Goldberg.

Permitted By Zoning Laws

It was learned from another source that North Suburban Synagog Beth El, of which Arnold P. Natenberg of Glencoe is president, contemplates using part of the Goldberg residence soon for religious services.

Carl Velde, chairman of the Highland Park zoning board of appeals, said a synagog could be erected in a single family residential neighborhood if off-the-street parking is provided on the lot or within 200 feet of the site at a ratio of one car for each eight persons seated in the main auditorium.

Comprises 7 1/2 Acres

The Goldberg property comprises 7 1/2 acres, with 480 feet of frontage on the lake. The house has 19 rooms, including a solarium which could seat several hundred persons, said Max Kunin, brother of Harry Kunin, a former owner of the property. The grounds were landscaped by the original owner, the late Ed V. Price, head of Ed V. Price & Co., wholesale tailors. According to Kunin the house cost about $750,-000. Goldberg said he paid slightly over $200,000 for the property.

Article appearing in the *Chicago Daily Tribune* on August 25, 1948, reporting on the purchase of "one of Highland Park's residential showplaces" by Max Goldberg for "slightly over $200,000" that may be used "for charitable or educational purposes, or for worship." (Chicago Tribune Archives)

The Bulletin of

NORTH SUBURBAN SYNAGOGUE BETH EL

1201 South Sheridan Road   Highland Park, Illinois

| VOL. 1 | OCTOBER 15, 1948 — TISHRI 12, 5709 | NO. 1 |

SUCCOTH SERVICES

Sunday, October 17, 8:00 P.M.
Monday, October 18, 9:30 A.M. and 4:30 P.M.
Tuesday, October 19, 9:30 A.M.

SHEMINI AZERET

Sunday, October 24, 8 P.M.
Monday, October 25, 9:30 A.M.
Yislon will be said during the Service.

SIMCHAT TORAH

Monday, October 25, 6:45 P.M.
Halsofoth (Torah Processions)
Our children will participate in and conduct the Service.
Tuesday, October 26, 9:30 A.M.

Rabbi Maurice I. Kliers will officiate.

Cantor Stanley Martin will chant the Service.

BETH EL SCHOOLS

Under the able direction of Mr. Meyer Shisler, Beth El is maintaining three schools: Gan or Nursery School, Hebrew School and Sunday School.

The aims of the Schools are threefold:

—To provide for our youth a wholesome Jewish atmosphere in which they may learn to live in accordance with the highest ideals of Judaism and Americanism.

—To enable our children to share Jewish experiences with a sense of joy, appreciation and creativity.

—To imbue in the Jew of tomorrow a deep sense of kinship and continuity with the Jewish past, and a keen desire to understand, appreciate and share the tasks of the Jewish future.

An intensive Jewish education for every Jewish child is our goal. Your child can be thoroughly happy with himself as a Jew only if he understands the heritage, the traditions, and the problems of his people.

Beth El Jewish Youth League

The League has been organized for all boys and girls who attend high school. Their purpose is to advance the Jewish cultural and social interests of its members. Paul Wolfe is president.

BAR MITZVAH

Gerson Meyers, son of Mr. and Mrs. Jonas Meyers, will become Bar Mitzvah on October 16, 1948, at our Synagogue.

Avrum Gray, the son of Mr. and Mrs. Joseph Gray, was the first to become Bar Mitzvah this year. The services took place on Saturday, September 18th at the Winnetka Women's Club.

The first Bar Mitzvah to be held in our new Synagogue was that of Allen Rubenstein, son of Mr. and Mrs. Louis Rubenstein.

Barry Briskman, son of Mr. and Mrs. Edwin H. Briskman, became Bar Mitzvah on October 9th at the North Shore Congregation Israel.

The Congregation wishes to extend to the B'nai Mitzvah and their Parents their sincerest congratulations.

RABBI'S DINNER

Some 170 people were present to greet Rabbi and Mrs. Kliers and Cantor Stanley Martin at a dinner given in their honor at the Ridgeview Hotel in Evanston. Mr. Joseph Gray capably chairmanned the affair. Invocation was given by Dr. Edgar Siskin and greetings by Milton Krensky, Arnold Natenberg, and Mrs. Oscar Pinsof. The program, including musical selections by the Cantor and dramatic presentations by Pearl Horand was deemed a most enjoyable and spirited gathering.

The Bulletin of North Suburban Synagogue Beth El, Volume 1, No. 1, dated October 15, 1948 - Tishri 12, 5709 edited by Ruth Shapiro. The address of the synagogue at that time was 1201 South Sheridan Road, Highland Park, Illinois. The present address of 1175 Sheridan Road took effect in 1951 when the City of Highland Park changed its street numbering system. (Beth El Archives)

This Indenture Witnesseth, that the Grantors,

MAX GOLDBERG and IDA GOLDBERG, his wife

of the City of Glencoe in the County of Cook

and State of Illinois for the consideration of TEN and no/100 Dollars

($10.00) and other good and valuable considerations — — — — — — — — — — Dollars,

Convey and Quit-Claim to NORTH SUBURBAN SYNAGOGUE BETH EL, an Illinois

Religious Corporation,

of the in the County of Cook and

State of Illinois all interest in the following described Real Estate,

to-wit: Lot One (1) in Ledgemere, being a subdivision of

part of Lot Three (3) in Birch's Resubdivision of

Blocks Eighty-Three (83), Eighty-four (84) and

Eighty-five (85), in the City of Highland Park,

according to the plat thereof recorded September

9, 1911, as document 137368, in Lake County, Ill.

situated in the County of Lake in the State of Illinois, hereby releasing
and waiving all rights under and by virtue of the Homestead Exemption Laws of the State of Illinois.

Witness the hand s and seals of the said grantors this 26th day

of November A. D. 19 48.

Max Goldberg [SEAL]

Ida Goldberg [SEAL]

[SEAL]

[SEAL]

Deed dated November 26, 1948 from Max and Ida Goldberg conveying the Price Estate to North Suburban Synagogue Beth El. The Goldberg's had purchased the property on behalf of the congregation in August, 1948. (Beth El Archives)

Rabbi Maurice Kliers (far left) stands with the first "Gan," the congregation's pre-school class, and the synagogue's green school bus in front of the Price mansion in the winter of 1948-1949. Stella Natenberg, representative of the Sisterhood which then had oversight of the synagogue's educational programs, is at the right. The author, Mort Steinberg, is the fifth child from the right; next to him is his brother Joseph and at the far right is Joy Blumberg, daughter of Harold and Ruby Blumberg. (Photo by Leonard Birnbaum; Beth El Archives)

The first wedding celebrated at Beth El was the marriage of Eliezer Krumbein to Elaine Frohman on June 18, 1950. Here, reviewing the *ketubah* (marriage contract) before the ceremony, are (L-R): Rabbi Maurice Kliers, Eliezer Krumbein, Cantor Robert Segal and Rabbi Edgar Siskin. (Courtesy of Eliezer Krumbein)

The wedding celebration for Phyllis Levin, the daughter of Arnold and Stella Natenberg, on August 20, 1950, in the backyard of the Price mansion overlooking Lake Michigan. (Courtesy of Phyllis Levin)

Beverly Rubenstein celebrates her "bas mitzvah" on Friday evening, October 20, 1950, the first bat mitzvah at Beth El. Coincidentally, Rabbi Philip L. Lipis had been invited to the synagogue for that *Shabbat* as a candidate for the position of rabbi. (L-R): Beverly Rubenstein, Cantor Stanley Martin, Rabbi Lipis. (Courtesy of Beverly Rubenstein Dratler)

INSTALLATION OF

RABBI PHILIP LIPIS

NORTH SUBURBAN SYNAGOGUE BETH EL

1175 Sheridan Road
Highland Park

SUNDAY JUNE 24, 1951
7:00 P. M.

PROGRAM
●

● RABBI SOLOMON GOLDMAN

Distinguished Scholar, Spiritual Leader of Anshe Emet and renowned Author will install our Rabbi.

His address will be a significant milestone in the history of our Congregation.

● Prominent and noted Rabbis and colleagues of our Rabbi will be our guests.

● After the ceremony the social festivities will start.

Our beautiful grounds overlooking the lake will be decorated and illuminated for your pleasure.

You will enjoy dancing under the stars and the date promises cool refreshing lake breezes.

———

(Over)

Philip L. Lipis was formally installed as the second senior rabbi of the congregation on June 24, 1951. Chaired by Maurice Kelner, the announcement invited members to dinner and dancing in "our beautiful grounds overlooking the lake" and noted "punch will be served in our 'Tea House on the cliff.'" Cost of admission was $7.50 per person. (Beth El Archives)

The Pompeian Fountain acquired in Europe by Edward V. Price and installed in a fish pond along the south wall of the sun parlor (now the Sager Beit HaMidrash) in the Price mansion. This room became the sanctuary of the congregation in 1948. Rabbi Lipis had the fountain and fish pond removed after Beth El was characterized in a local publication as a synagogue with its own baptismal font. (Beth El Archives)

The original design for the expansion of the synagogue's facilities prepared by architect Isadore Braun in 1952. (Beth El Archives)

The groundbreaking ceremony for the school building on September 14, 1952 included the installation of an engraved stone plaque imported from Israel. Here, Rabbi Philip L. Lipis (center, in dark suit) stands behind the plaque. On the far left is Isadore Braun, architect of the school building. (Photo by Edward Glover; Beth El Archives)

The newly completed school building in 1954. The engraved stone plaque installed two years earlier is visible to the right of the entrance. (Beth El Archives)

The groundbreaking ceremony on November 27, 1955 for the "community center," later to be dedicated as the Blumberg Auditorium, on the south lawn of the Price Estate. Standing (L-R): Max Rubenstein, Edward Glazier, synagogue president, Max Goldberg, Judy Perlman (for the Sunday School), Allen Gellman, Harold Blumberg, Isadore Braun (partially obstructed), Joseph Young (for the Hebrew School), Rabbi Philip L. Lipis and Al Joseph. In front are Scotty Fohrman (for the Nursery School) and Harry Hershman, School Director. (Photo by Leonard Birnbaum; Beth El Archives)

The *bimah* arranged for the first High Holiday services in the newly completed auditorium in 1957. (Photo by Leonard Birnbaum; Beth El Archives)

The "community center" building following its completion in 1957. It would remain in this condition, with its temporary wall displaying a menorah configured with concrete blocks, until construction of the Sanctuary commenced in 1961. (Photo by Leonard Birnbaum; Beth El Archives)

Rabbi Philip L. Lipis in uniform as a Lt. Commander in the U.S. Navy Reserve. Rabbi Lipis served as a chaplain with the Marine Corps in the Pacific during World War II and maintained his commitment to the Navy during the 1950s. (Beth El Archives)

NORTH SUBURBAN SYNAGOGUE
BETH EL BULLETIN

Rabbi: Philip L. Lipis

Cantor: Jordan H. Cohen

SPECIAL SANCTUARY CAMPAIGN EDITION No. 1

$160,000.00
PLEDGED
TO DATE

First fundraising brochure in 1959 for the campaign to build a new sanctuary. The design was created by architect Percival Goodman, who envisioned the structure to resemble a "jeweled crown." It would be two more years until adequate resources were at hand to commence construction of the Sanctuary. (Beth El Archives)

The Beth El choir in 1959 directed by Cantor Jordan Cohen. Standing (L-R): Jaye Lewitz, Benjamin Harris, Gertrude Harris, Bernard Sokol and Lorraine London. Seated (L-R): Hazel Robin, unidentified, Corky Eisner, Mildred Applebaum and Marge Birnbaum. (Times Photographers photo; Beth El Archives)

A planning session held in the living room of the Price mansion c.1960 for the construction of the Sanctuary. Standing (L-R): Albert Dolin, synagogue president, Isadore Finkelstein, Jerry Wein and Mel Stark. Seated (L-R): Bernard Zell, Isadore Braun, Benjamin Harris, Sheldon Kamin, Jerry Sternberg, Morris Lederman, Sol Shapiro and Cantor Jordan Cohen. (Photo by Percy N. Prior, Jr.; Beth El Archives)

Groundbreaking for the Sanctuary on June 11, 1961. (L-R): Harold Blumberg, Eli Field, synagogue president, Albert Dolin and Edward Glazier. (Beth El Archives)

U.S. Senator Everett Dirksen participated in the groundbreaking ceremony for the Sanctuary on June 11, 1961. Rabbi Philip L. Lipis and Eli Field, synagogue president, are pictured in the background. (Photo by Percy H. Prior, Jr.; Beth El Archives)

Construction of the Sanctuary continued through the winter of 1961-1962.
(Photo by Leonard Birnbaum; Beth El Archives)

A Board of Directors meeting in 1961. Until the completion of the Zell activity room, the directors met in the living room of the Price mansion, now the Maxwell Abbell Library. Seated at far right is Rabbi Philip L. Lipis; Eli Field, synagogue president, is on his right. The two women directors are (L–R) Rose Paset and Pearl White. (Photo by Percy N. Prior, Jr.; Beth El Archives)

NORTH SUBURBAN

SYNAGOGUE BETH EL

YOM HA MOREH

SABBATH SERVICE

HONORING

DR. LOUIS KATZOFF

1958-1963

FRIDAY, MAY 10th, 1963

✡

PHILLIP L. LIPIS, RABBI

JORDAN H. COHEN, CANTOR

Program for a special Friday night service on May 10, 1963 to honor Dr. Louis Katzoff on his fifth year as Educational Director at Beth El. Dr. Katzoff brought intense Hebrew education to the synagogue and he and his wife, Adina, made a major contribution to the educational and religious life of the congregation. (Beth El Archives)

NORTH SUBURBAN SYNAGOGUE BETH EL, 1175 SHERIDAN ROAD, HIGHLAND PARK, ILLINOIS

PROGRAM

Program from the formal dedication of the Sanctuary on November 27, 1964. Designed by architect Percival Goodman, the Sanctuary was first used for High Holiday services in 1962 but was not fully furnished until two years later. The entire *Shabbat* service on this occasion was led by members of the Youth Group. (Beth El Archives)

A "Passover Seder" for the Beth El pre-school c.1960s. (Beth El Archives)

The Sager Beit HaMidrash, following its renovation in 1967. (Beth El Archives)

January 3, 1968

Mr. Ben W. Sager, President
North Suburban Synagogue Beth El
239 Ivy Lane
Highland Park, Illinois

Dear Ben:

On June 6, 1930, I was ordained Rabbi, Teacher, and Preacher in Israel by the Jewish Theological Seminary of America. In the course of these nearly four decades of service in the American Rabbinate, I have served Beth El for nearly two decades, or for a period equal to the combined time I gave to three prior congregations and to the Chaplain Corps of the U. S. Navy.

During these years, it has been a source of pride and satisfaction to me to have participated with so many others in the development of a small, insecure congregation, unsure of itself and its future, into a strong, large, influential, prestigious congregation that is constantly bracketed with one or two others as the foremost Conservative Congregations in Chicagoland. I can honestly say that the years my family and I have been in Highland Park in association with Beth El, have been among the happiest, most creative, and most fulfilling of my career in the Rabbinate.

Most laymen are unaware of the enormous drain imposed on the time, energy, and thought of a Rabbi, who must prepare sermons, conduct services, carry on a heavy teaching load, serve as consultant to many committees and departments, act as counsellor and friend to multitudes in their sorrows, joys, and confusions, institute and develop new programs, chart new courses, actively engage in fund raising for Synagogue and worthwhile Jewish causes, and participate in the concerns of the larger community, general and Jewish. This far from exhausts the list of his duties.

These exacting burdens of constant activity and increasing pressures have led me to make an important and firm decision, after long reflection, soul searching, and careful deliberation. It is my considered opinion that the time has come for these responsibilities to pass on to a younger man who will bring youthful energies, fresh enthusiasm, and new ideas into the service of the congregation. My desire is to employ

Letter dated January 3, 1968 from Rabbi Philip L. Lipis to President Ben Sager advising that he wished "to be relieved of my duties as Rabbi of Beth El" prior to January 1, 1970. He and Shoshanah formally left the congregation following a testimonial dinner in their honor on July 13, 1969. (Beth El Archives)

Rabbi Philip L. Lipis and Beth El's presidents gather at the farewell testimonial dinner for the rabbi and Shoshanah Lipis on July 13, 1969. L-R: Max Applebaum, Albert Dolin, Harold Blumberg, Bernard Sokol, Rabbi Lipis, Edward Glazier, Eli Field, Harold Gorin and Ben Sager. (Salyards photo; Beth El Archives)

The Beth El choir in 1968 directed by Stanley Ackerman. Back row (L-R): Joe Klein, Ira Gur, Marge Birnbaum, Bernard Sokol and Morris Silberman. Third row (L-R): Joel Resnick, Elaine Lewin, Mary Gettelman, Jaye Lewitz and Gerald Goodman. Second row (L-R): Sonia Kass, Dorothy Liebenson and Iris Brenner. Front row (L-R): Gwen Cooper, Marlene Silberman and Sharon Levin. (Beth El Archives)

III. ENHANCING THE DREAM
(1969–1977)

At a special meeting of the Board of Directors on March 13, 1969, the Board approved the recommendation of the Rabbi Selection Committee, headed by past president Bernard Sokol, to call Rabbi Samuel H. Dresner of Springfield, Massachusetts to the pulpit.[88] Born in 1923 and raised on the north side of Chicago,[89] Rabbi Dresner had been raised in the liberal teachings of Reform Judaism, but while a student at Northwestern University had become a devotee of Abraham Joshua Heschel. He eventually followed Heschel first to the University of Cincinnati and then to New York and the Jewish Theological Seminary where he was ordained in 1951. Rabbi Dresner arrived at Beth El in August, 1969 and soon presented his agenda of strength in education, maintenance of high standards for Jewish living, and institutional development. An eloquent speaker and a noted scholar,[90] the congregation eagerly welcomed the rabbi, his wife Ruth, and their four daughters into the community.

The search for a new cantor took longer. Tevele Cohen, father of the late Jordan Cohen, had graciously and beautifully served as *hazzan* for the High Holidays in 1969.[91] Finally on April 30, 1970, after an arduous search, Joel Rabinowitz, chairman

---

[88]   When the pulpit of the congregation was declared vacant in accordance with the procedures of the Rabbinical Assembly, forty-four rabbis submitted their candidacy for the position, an occurrence unprecedented in the Conservative movement.

[89]   Dresner attended Senn High School where he was known as an outstanding athlete and earned the nick-name "King Kong Dresner."

[90]   Rabbi Dresner had authored several books before coming to Beth El and had been the editor of *Conservative Judaism* from 1955 to 1964; until 2010, this was the longest tenure of any editor of that scholarly journal. During his career, he would author a total of seventeen books and numerous articles.

[91]   Tevele Cohen was considered "the dean" of Chicago cantors and served Congregation Beth Itzchak of Albany Park for more than thirty years. He died in 1987 at the age of 92.

of the Cantor Selection Committee, recommended the selection of Cantor Reuven Frankel of Congregation Shaarey Zedek in Southfield, Michigan.[92] The recommendation was unanimously approved by the Board of Directors.

Although the spiritual leadership had changed during the preceding twelve months, the activities of the congregation had continued without interruption. Harold Gorin became president of the congregation in the spring of 1969 and oversaw numerous community events[93] as well as innovative programming at the synagogue. That year the Solomon Schechter Day School broke ground for the construction of its own facilities on Lee Road in Northbrook. The school had been founded in 1961 and for eight years had held classes at B'nai Emunah synagogue in Skokie and then at Beth Hillel Congregation in Wilmette. The day school had been one of Rabbi Lipis' most cherished projects and the synagogue Board annually had assisted it financially. In June of 1969, the congregation invited the Schechter School to utilize Beth El's school building until its own new facilities were completed. In 1970, complimentary one-year memberships in the congregation were first granted to newly married couples who were children of Beth El families so as to encourage their participation in synagogue life. Another milestone in the development of Beth El's educational programs occurred in the spring of 1970 when the School Board, under the direction of Elmer Burack, authorized the Melton Research Center to conduct a survey of the religious schools. This eventually led to the introduction of the Melton teacher training program and utilization of its advanced materials and programs to strengthen Beth El's educational system.

In an attempt to help defray increasing costs without raising dues, the Board of Directors authorized the implementation of

---

92   Cantor Frankel was born in the Meah Sharim neighborhood of Jerusalem in 1930 and came to this country in 1939. On *Shabbat* morning, February 12, 1966, he was on the *bimah* at Shaarey Zedek when Rabbi Morris Adler was shot and killed by a troubled young congregant.

93   In December, 1968, a new Conservative congregation, Beth Judea, was formed in Long Grove. President Gorin and the Executive Committee were quick to consult with the leadership of the new neighbor and to offer assistance and guidance to that synagogue.

the Graduated Dues Program in 1971. Based on the concept of voluntary dues in excess of the minimum requirement, the program proved very successful, raising over $80,000 in its first year, and it continued over the years as the Sustaining Membership Program and then as the Fair Share Dues Program. Also in 1971, the congregation, to signal its firm support for Israel, purchased $2 million in State of Israel Bonds by using the synagogue's property as collateral for a loan in that amount. This practice continued for over thirty-five years until bonds of that type were no longer offered by Israel.

As the congregation matured, familiar faces who had been with the synagogue for many years inevitably moved on to new endeavors. Dr. Louis Katzoff, who had served as educational director for thirteen years, retired in the summer of 1971 at the age of sixty-three. He and Adina were honored at the synagogue's annual dinner dance that June. They soon moved to Jerusalem but continued to stay in touch with their many close friends in Highland Park, often returning at the request of the congregation to assist in the rabbinic duties on the High Holidays. Their apartment on King David Street in Jerusalem was always open to Beth El families visiting Israel. Mr. Samuel Skidelsky, the "dean" of Beth El teachers, also announced his retirement after eighteen years with the school.[94] He, too, made *aliyah* to Jerusalem. The congregation mourned the passing of both of these men of scholarship and distinction in 1987.[95]

By the early 1970s, the rush of population to Highland Park began to subside as many Jewish families with young children began moving to the "new" suburbs centered in and around Buffalo Grove.[96] Although congregational membership reached 850 in October, 1971, student enrollment numbered only 636 and would continue dropping to below 500 over the next several

---

[94] To honor Mr. Skidelsky on his retirement, the synagogue invited his former students to write letters of appreciation to their former teacher which were then presented to him in the form of a tribute book.

[95] After the death of Dr. Katzoff, his wife, Adina, continued to reside in Jerusalem, the city in which she was born. She passed away in May, 2018, at the age of 104.

[96] See footnote number 93.

years. Yet the school continued its commitment to a strong educational program. Rabbi David Saltzman, who had succeeded Dr. Katzoff as educational director in 1971, left the congregation in 1973. The search committee for a new educational director, co-chaired by Irving Rozenfeld and David Weinstein, recommended Binyamin Markovitz of Port Jefferson, New York, who was retained in April, 1973.

Daniel Tauman was elected president of the congregation in 1971 and one of his first acts was to recommend the purchase of the residence at 1232 Sheridan Road to be the "parsonage" (later called the "rabbinic residence") for the congregation's rabbi. The house had first been rented for use by Rabbi Dresner and his family upon their arrival in 1969. Soon after its purchase, an extensive remodeling of the house was made under the supervision of Ed Gettleman, chairman of the House Committee. Also in 1971, Cyril Oldham left his position as executive director and was replaced by Mel Karp of Philadelphia, Pennsylvania.

The impact of the leadership of Rabbi Dresner was now being realized. In his annual report delivered to the congregation in June, 1972, President Tauman noted that "Shabbat morning services have consistently been well attended bringing out no less than 350 and as many as 600 participants, many of whom are young adults." The concern of the congregation was focused on the plight of Russian Jewry and a "Save Soviet Jews" sign was placed on the synagogue grounds alongside Sheridan Road, where it would remain for the next two decades until the breakup of the Soviet Union in the early 1990s. In October, 1972, over 120 *sukkot* were constructed in the community. Under the direction of Eliezer Krumbein and the new youth director, Hillel Kliers (son of Beth El's first rabbi, Maurice Kliers), Y.E.L.P. (Youth Education Leadership Program) was instituted and continued successfully for a number of years. The following year, the school implemented the Halomdim Program, so that children with diagnosed learning disabilities would not be deprived of a Jewish education.[97]

---

[97] The Halomdim Program, which continues to the present, would be endowed by Cal and Lana Eisenberg, longtime members of the synagogue.

In the area of education and religious commitment, Beth El thrived. But the general economic recession of the early 1970s also impacted the congregation. Increased costs compelled dues to be increased to $450 in 1972 and membership in the congregation dropped to 739 families by late that year.

Two men were honored at a State of Israel Bonds Testimonial Dinner in the Blumberg Auditorium on November 2, 1972. More than anyone else, Sol Shapiro, who had been with Beth El from its inception, and Isadore Finkelstein had been the backbone of ritual observance since the early days of the congregation, organizing the daily *minyan*, supervising *Shabbat* services, collecting *maot chitim* each Passover, and lovingly and devotedly performing other important functions in the religious life of the community. They were well-deserved recognitions.

1973 was another eventful year. In March, Paul and Miriam Rosenblum dedicated the synagogue's library in memory of Miriam's father, Maxwell Abbell, a stalwart of the Chicago Jewish community and a prominent figure in the Conservative movement for many years.[98] The next month Mel Karp left the synagogue and in June Sam Rade, a longtime member of the congregation, was hired as the new executive director, a position he held with great effectiveness and devotion for the next twelve years. The Zell Activity Room was dedicated in June by the Board of Directors in honor of the generosity of Rochelle and Bernard Zell. Albert Kopin, Ritual Vice President, announced the institution of an early *kabbalat Shabbat* service during the summer months and it soon replaced the traditional late Friday night services. As the congregation prepared to celebrate its twenty-fifth anniversary, Leonard Birnbaum wrote an extensive history of the synagogue's first quarter of a century and Sisterhood dedicated a series of five beautiful tapestries depicting different aspects of Jewish community life. The tapestries were designed by artist Ina Golub of New Jersey, who

---

[98] In June, 1958, the library had been moved into its "new" quarters in what previously was the dining room of the Price mansion and which today is the Pinsof Children's Reading Room. Since 1973, the Maxwell Abbell Library has been located in the former living room of the Price mansion.

had been chosen for this project several years earlier at the time Zella Ludwig[99] served as Sisterhood president. They were then meticulously handcrafted by Sisterhood members under the guidance of Judy Sarnat and were displayed prominently in the sanctuary foyer.[100]

After twenty-five years, Beth El had achieved a reputation for innovative Jewish education, traditional religious observance and a strong commitment to the Jewish community. It fulfilled social as well as spiritual needs of over 2,000 individuals. It had been successful in the development of a large number of committed young people who would be able to assume roles of leadership in the Jewish community. Rabbi Lipis, now retired in California but still recognized as the force which had helped build the congregation during his tenure in Highland Park, was invited to share a twenty-fifth anniversary message with the congregation. After noting with deserved pride the many achievements of the congregation through its first quarter of a century, he concluded with his hope for the future:

> Shoshanah and I pray that, under the spiritual leadership of Rabbi Dresner who has been my successor these four years, under the dedicated lay leadership that will continue to uphold his hands, and with the support of the congregation as a whole, there will open up for Beth El a new chapter of fresh growth and achievement on which will be recorded added glory to the name of God, increase of honor to Torah and the spread of light and healing to our people everywhere. Amen.

As the congregation observed Yom Kippur in 1973, it was astounded by the news of the invasion of Israel by Egypt. Although in need of funds for the synagogue, the leadership of

99   Zella Ludwig, a member of the congregation since 1957, would be an important influence in the Beth El community for many years, eventually becoming a member of the Board of Trustees. She passed away in 2016.

100   At the time of the renovation of the corridor around the Field Family Sanctuary in 2016, these tapestries were removed and scheduled to be relocated to the Natkin Seminar Room in the school building.

the congregation, now headed by President Melvin Pollack, never wavered in its concerted effort to support the Jewish state during the tense days of the Yom Kippur War. Within two months, over $560,000 had been contributed by Beth El members to the Israel Emergency Fund, and that was in addition to the $965,000 contributed by them that year to the regular Jewish United Fund campaign.

In March, 1974, the congregation was honored to hear a series of lectures by Elie Wiesel. His visit was due to the personal efforts of Rabbi Dresner and Ronald and Ethel Taub. 1974 also witnessed a significant change in religious practice at the synagogue.[101] Rabbi Dresner advised the congregation of the recommendation of the Rabbinical Assembly that women be included in constituting a *minyan* and be permitted to participate in the Torah service. Sensing that this was historically proper and in keeping with *halacha*, the rabbi instituted that policy starting in January, 1974. At the same time, Friday night *b'not mitzvah*, which long had been the standard practice at Beth El and many other congregations, were eliminated, thereafter to be celebrated on *Shabbat* morning. The first girls to participate in this new policy were Ranna Rozenfeld and Judith Wexler, cousins who read from the Torah at their joint bat mitzvah in 1974.

By that time, Membership Chairman Seymour Siegel reported to the Board that membership had once again begun to grow, reaching 775 families. As part of an effort to keep the directors and congregants advised of the myriad of important activities being provided by the auxiliary institutions, President Pollack asked for in-depth reports from each group. In September, Joseph Ament reported on the activities of the Couples Club in the areas of study, social programs and development of a sense of *havurah*. In succeeding months, Joyce Pollack, in a beautiful report entitled "Who, What, Why and How of Your Sisterhood,"

---

101   During this time Bernie Alpert led a group of congregants in attempting to provide an *eruv* for Highland Park. The idea met with resistance from public officials and could not be implemented. An *eruv* encompassing much of Highland Park, including Beth El, was finally established in about 2010, with the assistance of Rabbi Yossi Schanowitz of the Central Avenue Synagogue (Lubavitch-Chabad).

reported on the endless programs and achievements of Sisterhood and Gerald Schur described the activities and goals of the Men's Club.

Congregational life was hectic, active and progressive. In 1975, after years of planning, a separate High Holiday Family Service was instituted at the Highland Park High School auditorium. Dr. Katzoff returned from Israel to lead that service. The Mom and Me program became part of the nursery school activities in 1976, the same year that Sisterhood published its best-selling cookbook, *Tradition in the Kitchen.*[102] Jean Bernstein and Eenie Frost even appeared on television to share favorite Passover recipes from the book with the community! In May of 1977, the congregation heard the world-renowned tenor Jan Peerce perform at the Highland Park High School auditorium, a concert remembered by all who attended as being warm and delightful.

Yet throughout this period, a growing discontent cast a shadow over the synagogue. Within a few years after Rabbi Dresner's arrival, many congregants sensed a difficulty in communicating with him on a personal level, and others perceived a lack of involvement on his part in pastoral duties and administrative and other functions of the synagogue. Between 1971 and 1977, numerous liaison committees were established by the presidents to facilitate better understanding between the rabbi and a large segment of the congregation. These committees, chaired successively by Eli Field, Harold Gorin and Joel Rabinowitz, noted the rabbi's important contributions to the congregation, yet found serious deficiencies and detected little change in the areas of concern held by a growing number of congregants.

The increasing pressure to resolve the conflict soon reached a climax. At a special meeting of the Board of Directors held on March 2, 1977, to which the entire congregation had been invited by President Larry Tayne, a motion not to renew the employment of Rabbi Dresner at the end of his contract period on June 30 of that year was approved by a vote of forty-six in favor, ten opposed.

---

102   Eenie Frost and Maxine Greenstein were editors of the book, with Jean Bernstein, Rachel Weiss, Evelyn Aronson, Dorothy Kanes and Sarah Stiebel serving on the editorial staff.

The congregation was in turmoil. Those who supported the retention of the rabbi formed "The Committee For The Preservation Of North Suburban Synagogue Beth El." They quickly circulated a petition to nominate their own slate of officers and directors who were pledged to retain the rabbi. Included among them were men and women who for years had devotedly served the congregation. M.D. "Mush" Oberman headed the slate; others included Edgar Gettleman, Joe Davis, Sonia Bloch, Sherman Corwin, Herman DeKoven, Herman Finch,[103] Arthur Sherman and Leonard Zieve. These candidates would oppose the slate prepared by the Congregational Nominating Committee in the only contested election in the history of Beth El.

The election meeting of the congregation was set for Sunday, April 12, 1977. In the weeks before, letters and offers of mediation came from the highest levels of the Jewish Theological Seminary in New York.[104] An intense publicity campaign by mail was undertaken by the supporters of the rabbi. The Sisterhood and Men's Club wrote letters urging the election of the candidates supporting the action of the Board. The Board invited the congregation to a series of two "Town Hall" meetings to explain the reasons for its action.

On the day of the election, the "polls" opened at 2:00 p.m. in the Blumberg Auditorium. Voting was by secret ballot and only after each member had presented proper identification to election judges and had been verified as being current in his or her financial obligations to the synagogue. The vote was supervised and officially tallied by an outside independent accounting firm. 1,215 votes were recorded. When it was over, the slate proposed by the Congregational Nominating Committee had

---

[103]   Finch, for probably twenty years, had been the regular *baal t'kiya* for the congregation on the High Holidays. After he left Beth El in the summer of 1977, Morton Steinberg would sound the shofar yearly, with very few exceptions, at Rosh Hashanah services.

[104]   One letter from the Seminary, signed by twelve members of the faculty and the Executive Vice-President of the Rabbinical Assembly, characterized the Board's decision as *"hilul hashem,"* profaning God's name. Dr. Gerson Cohen, Chancellor of the Seminary, quickly wrote his own letter to the congregation clarifying that this did "not represent Seminary policy, officially or unofficially."

received more than sixty-six percent of the votes.

The contested election opened a wound in the congregation. It tore apart relationships that had been formed during the better part of a generation. Congregants who had once been close friends ceased talking with each other. Men and women who for years had worshiped together and had worked side by side dissolved their bonds of friendship. Within a matter of days, the leadership of the rabbi's supporters announced plans to establish a new Conservative congregation, Moriah, in Deerfield. In August, Rabbi Dresner became its first spiritual leader.[105]

In the aftermath of the tensions and strife caused by the contested election, the congregation was stunned by tragic news. On April 26, 1977, Rabbi Lipis died from injuries suffered in an automobile accident in California. His funeral was held on April 29 in the sanctuary which he had struggled for so many years to build. Mournfully, the congregation gathered: young adults whom he had helped guide in the traditions of the Jewish people; founders who had shared with him dreams and sorrows and triumphs; new congregants who had known of him more by reputation than by personal acquaintance. They, together with the many friends and colleagues who spoke at the service, among them Dr. Simon Greenberg, Vice Chancellor of the Jewish Theological Seminary, Rabbi David Polish of Chicago, and his good friend and neighbor Rabbi Sholom Singer of Congregation B'nai Torah in Highland Park, bid a final farewell to the beloved Philip L. Lipis.[106]

---

105   Greatly embittered by the result of the congregation's vote, for many years after leaving Beth El Rabbi Dresner, perhaps understandably, refused to speak with any of its professionals or members. He served as the rabbi of Moriah until 1984, when he returned to teach at the Jewish Theological Seminary in New York. He passed away in 2000.

106   For several years preceding his death, Rabbi Lipis had collaborated with Dr. Katzoff on writing a book based upon weekly Torah commentaries they had prepared while at Beth El. *Torah For the Family* was published by the World Jewish Bible Society shortly after Rabbi Lipis' death. Following his death, Shoshanah Lipis moved back to the Chicago community. In 1979, she married Louis Winer, one of the giants of the Conservative movement. Shoshanah Lipis Winer, as she was thereafter known, passed away on May 27, 1993. Her funeral was held at Beth El three days later.

IV. THE DREAM RENEWED
(1977–1987)

In May, 1977, Howard Lidov became the new president of Beth El and acted quickly to put the events of that spring behind the congregation. Despite the problems that faced the synagogue, its members were bolstered by Eli Field's reminder that "the Torah would still be read" at Beth El. Alex Knopfler was appointed to head a Transition Committee to help heal the rift within the congregation. Later in the year, the Board of Directors approved arbitration, with Daniel Tauman acting on behalf of the synagogue, as the means to settle all financial issues with Rabbi Dresner, a process which would not be concluded until four years later.

Attention was once again turned to continuing the strength of the synagogue's programming and educational system. In June, 1977, Marvin Kassof was hired as the new educational director and David Kupperstock joined the congregation as youth director. The same month Carole Golin became the new director of the nursery school. She would continue in that position for a decade, building the nursery school program into one of the finest on the North Shore.

As in its earliest years, Beth El was without its own rabbi for the High Holidays in 1977. Rabbi Stanley Schachter, Vice-Chancellor of the Jewish Theological Seminary and formerly rabbi of Ner Tamid Congregation in Chicago, was invited to officiate and he, along with Dr. Katzoff, who again traveled from Israel, conducted services. Despite more than 100 resignations from the membership rolls that summer due to the rift caused by the departure of Rabbi Dresner, Morton Bernstein, chairman of the Membership Committee, was able to report following the High Holidays that total membership had actually risen to 783 families.

Soon plans were formulated to celebrate Beth El's thirtieth

anniversary. Jack Frost undertook responsibility for this event and on March 21, 1978 an "Etz Chaim," a Tree of Life, located close to the Sager Bet HaMidrash was dedicated by Rabbi Ralph Simon of Congregation Rodfei Zedek in Chicago. The honor of unveiling this new dedication was accorded to Benjamin and Gertrude Harris, whose vision and hard work had helped establish the congregation thirty years earlier.[107]

Throughout the winter and spring of 1978, the congregation's attention was focused on finding a new spiritual leader. At a special meeting of the Board of Directors on June 1, 1978, former president Mel Pollack, chairman of the Rabbi Search Committee, recommended bringing Rabbi William H. Lebeau of Port Jefferson, New York to the pulpit. The recommendation was unanimously approved.

Rabbi Lebeau, a native of Akron, Ohio, was born in 1938. After spending a summer at Camp Ramah in Wisconsin as a waiter and junior counselor, he transferred from the University of Akron to New York University in order to study at the Jewish Theological Seminary, where he was ordained in 1964. Like Rabbi Lipis before him, he had served as a chaplain in the U.S. Navy, based in San Diego. Rabbi Lebeau, Beverly and their five children visited the Beth El community that summer and he first took the pulpit at *Shabbat* services on the morning of August 26, 1978. However, due to commitments to his prior congregation, he was unable to officiate for the High Holidays. Services for Rosh Hashanah and Yom Kippur that fall were led by Rabbi Neil Gilman of the Jewish Theological Seminary and Rabbi Marc Tannenbaum, the noted human rights and social justice activist.

1979 was scheduled to start with a gala installation ceremony for Rabbi Lebeau, arranged by Yadelle Sklare for January 14, but the event was cancelled due to a severe blizzard. It was rescheduled for April 8 and took place despite fears that it would again have to be postponed due to the emergency surgery needed

---

107   The Etz Chaim dedication was removed and placed in storage in the 1980s to permit the installation of additional memorial tablets. It has remained in storage since then.

by the rabbi that spring. Dr. Simon Greenberg, Vice-Chancellor of the Seminary, and the rabbi's brother, Rabbi James Lebeau, addressed the congregation at that joyous event.

As the congregation welcomed its new rabbi, it said goodbye to its cantor. Reuven Frankel had received rabbinic ordination from the Hebrew Theological College in Skokie in 1976. In May of 1979 he left Beth El to become the first spiritual leader of Congregation B'nai Tikvah in Deerfield. A special *oneg Shabbat* was held in honor of Reuven and Penina in April. Throughout the years, they maintained a continuing friendship with the professional leadership and membership of Beth El.[108] Through the efforts of the Cantor Search Committee, chaired by former president Harold Gorin, Eliahu Treistman became the new cantor in June, 1979. Cantor Triestman, a graduate of the Tel Aviv Academy of Music, was born in Bessarabia in 1933 and immigrated to Israel after World War II. He came to the United States following service in the Israeli air force. He had served as cantor at synagogues in New Jersey and New York. That same month Beth Cohen became the new youth director of the synagogue.

As the congregation began to get to know its new rabbi, activities at the synagogue continued. In February, 1979, the Men's Club, under the leadership of Phil Zand, instituted its first Blood Drive; it would become an annual event. At Purim, Michael Katz read *Megilat Esther* in the Sager Bet HaMidrash in his inimitable style, a tradition which continues to the present.[109] At Passover, Milt Fields,[110] following in the footsteps of his father, Isadore Finkelstein, collected *maot chitim*, not only for Beth El but on behalf of the Greater Chicago Maot Chittim

---

[108]   Reuven Frankel served as rabbi at B'nai Tikvah until his retirement in 1999. He passed away in 2013. Penina soon rejoined the Beth El community.

[109]   Katz, in his chanting of the *megilah*, instituted over the years what may be a custom unique to Beth El: after each mention of the name of Haman's wife, Zeresh, he added, and soon the whole congregation joined him in adding, an emphatic "Feh!"

[110]   Milt Fields had joined Beth El in 1952 and remained active in the *maot chitim* program as well as in synagogue affairs until his death in 2010. The duration of his membership, 58 years, was one of the longest of any member of Beth El.

fund. Laurie Benjamin and Amos Turner of the House Committee prepared a list of major structural repairs required to be undertaken in the mansion building, which by then was almost seventy years old. The work was eventually accomplished the following year under the capable supervision of Julian Saper. Throughout that year, and continuing for many years to come, Myrna Schwartz lovingly prepared beautiful exhibits for the Kol Ami Museum. In June, 1979, Reverend Kornfeld retired after twelve years of devoted service to the congregation, although he and Ruth would remain active in the Beth El family for many years thereafter.[111] The synagogue was without a ritual administrator until the following year, when a search committee, chaired by Morton Steinberg, recommended hiring Harry Halbkram of White Plains, New York, to fill that position.[112]

Arnold Kaplan succeeded Howard Lidov as president of the congregation in May, 1979. He soon was faced with the first significant controversy involving Rabbi Lebeau. The rabbi had made it clear that he would not officiate at any wedding unless it was followed by a kosher meal. Some members strongly criticized this policy and threatened to resign unless it was rescinded. But when the issue was brought to the Board of Directors, the rabbi's position was strongly supported. Only four families left the synagogue due to this issue.

By October, 1979 membership in the congregation had increased to 812 families. Arthur Rubinoff, Vice President Finance, undertook a memorable project to raise funds for the increasing budget: the congregation would write its own Torah. Through a series of meetings in members' homes, more than $78,000 was raised for the Torah-writing project. On June 15, 1980, a beautiful *siyyum* was held at the synagogue at which the scribe, Rabbi Moshe Klein, completed his task before the congregation. The event was organized by Leonard Birnbaum, who also prepared

---

111   Reverend Kornfeld passed away in 1991 and was buried in Israel. His wife, Ruth, continued to be part of the Beth El community until she died in 2003.

112   Upon their arrival at Beth El, Harry and Linda Halbkram took up residence in the coach house. It has since served as the home for all subsequent ritual directors.

a symbolic Torah scroll commemorating this event which is on permanent display in the sanctuary foyer. Also in 1979, Rabbi Lebeau, recognizing the importance of maintaining Jewish ties to college-aged children of members, instituted annual visits to university campuses in the Midwest so as to remain in touch with this important segment of the congregation.

In the summer of 1980, Judy Light was hired to serve as both the new youth director and as program director for the growing congregation. That same month Cantor Treistman left the congregation and for a year the congregation was without the services of a permanent cantor. For the High Holidays that fall, Cantor Jacob Barkin was invited to chant the liturgy in the main sanctuary. By then the growing number of committed Jewish families in Highland Park was making an impact on the community. A strictly kosher delicatessen, Selig's, had opened for business, and in September it was announced that a Lubavitch Chabad House would soon be opening.[113]

The search for a permanent cantor continued and in January 1981, Robert Berger, chairman of the Cantor Search Committee, recommended hiring Cantor Aryeh Finklestein of Congregation Kol Emeth in Skokie. The cantor's arrival necessitated additional housing and the house at 1241 Lincoln Avenue South was purchased for his use. As the new cantor joined the community, Marvin Kassof, the educational director who had served for four years, announced he had taken a position at Congregation Shaarey Zedek in Southfield, Michigan. Ruth Belzer chaired the committee which quickly brought Dorothy Wexler to the position of Director of Education from Congregation Solel in Highland Park. At the same time, Ritual Vice President Norman Levinsohn obtained the services of William Weisel to serve as cantor for the Family Services at the Highland Park High School for the fall of 1981. Since then Cantor Weisel, even after he moved with his family to Israel, has, except for 1993, returned annually to fill that position.

---

[113] The Chabad House slowly grew over the years, eventually constructing its own facility, the Central Avenue Synagogue, in the mid-1990s which included a *mikvah* open to the entire Jewish community.

In the spring of 1981, Rabbi Lebeau led the congregation in one of the rarest of Jewish religious ceremonies: *Birkat Hachama*, the Blessing of the Sun, which occurs only once every twenty-eight years. On April 8 of that year, a Wednesday, corresponding to the 4th of Nissan 5741, the morning *minyan* gathered for services in the synagogue's backyard, and although the sky was cloudy, the sun, for just a moment, shone through the clouds at the proper time so that the appropriate blessings could be recited.[114]

In June, 1981, Laverne Isaacson retired. For almost twenty-five years she had devotedly served Beth El as administrator of its religious school and had been a warm and sympathetic advisor to two generations of students and parents. She soon moved to California, where she passed away in 1985.

Dorothy Wexler brought renewed leadership to the religious school and over the years the school developed a well-deserved reputation for excellence in Hebrew education. However, the Hebrew High School, which was operated under the auspices of the Chicago Board of Jewish Education, was no longer meeting at Beth El due to a lack of classrooms. In September, 1981, the Board of Directors, now led by President Albert Kopin, approved a total renovation of the second floor of the mansion building at a cost of $100,000 to create acceptable school facilities. By the fall of 1982, after completion of the work, Beth El once again housed the community Hebrew High School with an enrollment of over 100 teenagers.

In conjunction with the renovations for the school, the congregation realized that the main sanctuary, which had served as a house of worship for twenty years, was in need of remodeling. A committee headed by Mae Spitz undertook the total recarpeting and refurnishing of the sanctuary in the summer of 1982. The job was completed before Rosh Hashanah and below budget!

The multitude of programs increased pressures on the synagogue's budget, which exceeded $1 million for the first time in

---

114 Rabbi Kurtz had the privilege of leading the celebration of *Birkat Hachama* twenty-eight years later on April 8, 2009, which coincided with *erev Pasach*, Passover eve.

1982. Several fundraising events were undertaken. In January 1983, under the chairmanship of Jeffrey Wohlstadter, Cantor Aryeh Finklestein was joined by his brother, Cantor Meir Finklestein of Los Angeles, for a sell-out *Shabbat Shira* concert in the Blumberg Auditorium. It was an evening of utmost beauty. Shortly afterward, former president Mel Pollack headed up the "Thank you Beth El" campaign, which raised money in recognition of the many services the synagogue had provided to its membership over the years.

At the time the renovation to the synagogue's facilities was undertaken in 1982, consideration was first given to a new campaign to raise $750,000 for the cost of other urgently needed capital repairs. At the same time, the bonds of close personal affection were growing between the congregation and its rabbi. Through contacts at religious services, the popular *Vav* classes for bar and bat mitzvah children and their parents, weddings, funerals, ceremonies of *brit mila*, conversion classes and an occasional *pidyon haben*, individual members came to admire and love Rabbi Lebeau for his sensitivity, compassion, conviction and warm sense of humor. The rabbi perceived the need for a major undertaking to implement new and vital programs in the community. The need for improved facilities and enhanced programming came together during 1983. In January, Rabbi Lebeau presented a paper to the Board of Directors entitled "Need for Evaluation," reviewing his four-and-one-half-year relationship with the congregation and setting forth his personal agenda for areas of growth. This was followed by his "Proposal for Cultural and Learning Center," a new facility which would create a "unique area for the encouragement of Jewish studies by adults and children." He also presented his concept of an intensive youth program, to be known as the Youth Community, to the Board of Education. And he actively continued to promote the enrollment of the synagogue's youth in Camp Ramah, which he acknowledged had been a transformative experience in his own life.

The leadership of the congregation quickly joined forces to implement the rabbi's vision. Glen Bernfield, the initial chair of the fundraising effort, outlined a plan to raise $3.5 million. A professional fundraising coordinator was hired for this most ambitious of all Beth El campaigns. Under new President Gerald Buckman, a committee was formed to provide leadership for the new Capital Fund and Endowment Campaign, initially under the chairmanship of Alex Knopfler. By September, 1983, the details of the Campaign, including commemorative and endowment gift opportunities, were approved by the Board. The slogan of the Campaign was *"Mai-dor l'dor,"* From Generation to Generation; it recognized that just as the original founders of the synagogue had provided for their children, so too did the current generation have the obligation to provide its children with the facilities and programs which would create a strong house of worship, fellowship and study. For at least one family, that slogan became a reality the following May when Gerald Blumberg, whose birth had been noted in the very first synagogue bulletin some thirty-six years earlier, became a member of the Board of Directors.[115]

At Rosh Hashanah services during the fall of 1983, Rabbi Lebeau's sermon was entitled "North Suburban Synagogue Beth El – The Future." He spoke to the entire congregation of his dream:

> There is only one Jewish communal institution – the synagogue – that has the urgent goal of the transmission of our religious heritage as its *raison d'etre*....Because of the seriousness of this moment in Jewish life, the question must be asked of our synagogue: Are our facilities and programs adequate to meet our responsibility to the future?

The enthusiasm for the Campaign gained momentum. One of the first major contributions was the gift of the family of first and second-generation members Joseph and Ethel Horwitz and David and Barbara Hoffman, who dedicated the Horwitz/Hoffman Youth Lounge. By May, 1984, even before the formal

---

115 Gerald's father, Harold, had not lessened his commitment to Beth El. He attended the Board meetings that considered the new Campaign and strongly supported that endeavor.

Campaign had been presented to the congregation, over $700,000 had been pledged.

While these exciting events were unfolding, more changes were taking place. The office of Financial Secretary was created by the Board of Directors to ensure that no one would be denied membership in the congregation because of financial hardship. Daniel Hoseman was the first to hold that office, and he served with distinction for three years. By the spring of 1983, membership in the congregation had grown to 950 families and a committee headed by Joseph Betensky sought an assistant rabbi to ease the burden under which Rabbi Lebeau labored. That summer, Rabbi Sam Fraint of Cliffside Park, New Jersey, became the first to hold that position at Beth El. His arrival necessitated additional housing for the growing professional staff and the synagogue purchased the condominium townhouse at 750 Judson Avenue for Rabbi Fraint, his wife, Deena, and their young family.

In January, 1984, the architectural firm of Bernheim and Kahn was retained to prepare plans for construction of the new facilities. The plans included turning the entire first floor of the mansion building [116] into a new Cultural and Learning Center, which would include the existing Maxwell Abbell Library. Also contemplated was a new multi-purpose room to be constructed between the mansion and the school building. The school itself would be renovated and enlarged by the addition of five new classrooms and new school offices. An entire new wing was to be built to house the large administrative staff as well as new offices for the rabbi, cantor, executive director and other professionals. Also included were plans for a new pre-school (no longer the "nursery" school) playground, an enlarged kitchen and additional storage facilities. It was a grand plan, intended to prepare Beth El for continued growth and excellence well into the 21st century.

---

[116] Following the construction of the auditorium, the Price mansion was often referred to as the "administration building" since the dining room was used first as the library and then as the synagogue office; the kitchen and butler's pantry, now the Lederman Art Room, were divided into several small offices; and the breakfast room, now the Susan Fisher Glick Memorial Research Center (the computer room), became the executive director's office.

In March, 1984, taking the first step to implement the rabbi's plan for improved programming, Sheila Radman Balk of St. Louis was hired as the first Youth Community Director.[117] In June of that year, both Cantor Finkelstein and Harry Halbkram left the congregation.[118] Again the congregation would be without a permanent cantor for another year; Cantor David Levine was invited to officiate at the High Holidays that autumn, and Alan Weiner of Worcester, Massachusetts was hired as the new ritual director. He and his wife Linda soon became welcomed friends to the congregation. In July, Norman Levinsohn, now Vice President Administration, hired George Zawislanski as the new building manager, who would serve the congregation devotedly until his death in 2001. In the fall, the Couples Club changed its name to the Beth El Havurah ("Fellowship") in recognition of its goals and its growing number of single members. That October also witnessed the Blumberg Auditorium overflowing with congregants, visitors and television reporters as the synagogue's Social Action Committee, under the leadership of Hilda Reingold, hosted a debate between Paul Simon and Charles Percy, candidates for United States Senator. 1984 also saw annual dues reach $1,000, as the Board sought to keep the congregation on a sound financial footing in light of a growing staff and growing inflation.

The Capital Fund and Endowment Campaign continued its progress. In September, 1984, former president Al Kopin assumed the responsibilities of chairman of the Campaign Committee. Committed to fiscal responsibility, he made it clear that construction would not start unless all necessary funds were on hand or pledged. Working closely with him were Fundraising Co-Chairs Richard Janger and Edith Kaye. Also,

117 In June, 1984, at Fink Park in Highland Park, the USY group reinstituted a student vs. staff (including officers) softball game. Despite President Buckman going four for four on behalf of "Lebeau's Lions," the USYers won the game.

118 With the departure of Cantor Finkelstein, the residence at 1241 Lincoln Avenue South was sold. However, the synagogue initially failed to cancel the landscaping contract for the property. When gardeners showed up to cut the grass and trim the bushes without payment, the new owners, a Russian immigrant family, exclaimed: "America! What a wonderful country!"

David Hoffman diligently and professionally served as chairman of the Architectural Committee and, working with Mae Spitz, developed essential plans for the new facilities. After much deliberation, building plans were approved, Campaign materials were prepared, and by January, 1985 pledges and gifts exceeded $1 million. In February, the Board of Directors, in recognition of the generosity of the family of Eli and Dina Field, declared the main sanctuary to be the Field Family Sanctuary. A formal dedication was held on September 22, 1985. How fitting that the house of worship which Eli had worked so hard to build twenty years earlier would bear the name of his family! Later that year, Sisterhood, under President Cara Madansky, followed a tradition established thirty years earlier by donating new kitchen facilities.[119]

Along with the fundraising went the planning for the programs. In April, the Board approved the synagogue's participation in the new SKIP (Send a Kid to Israel Partnership) program in a joint effort with the Jewish Federation of Chicago, thoroughly negotiated on behalf of Beth El by Howard Turner.[120] Soon after, Lois Janger was appointed to chair the committee to develop the new Cultural and Learning Center, which later would be dedicated by Joseph and Mae Gray, among the original founders of the congregation.

At the start of 1985, Sam Rade retired. He had served as executive director since 1973 and the Board of Directors voted him and Charlotte a life membership in the congregation. First Jerome Sternberg and then Gerald Goodman,[121] longtime members of the congregation, filled that position effectively on

---

[119] The Sisterhood donated in excess of $150,000 over the course of the Capital Fund and Endowment Campaign! Rabbi Lebeau often expressed great satisfaction in working with the strong lay leadership of the congregation, especially with the Sisterhood, which he considered a critical component of the Beth El community.

[120] The basic concept of the SKIP program, in which an institution would help fund an approved youth trip to Israel based upon the recipient's achievement of specified educational goals, initially had been a key element of Rabbi Lebeau's vision for the Beth El Youth Community.

[121] Goodman, a veteran of WWII, had landed with the first wave of Americans to assault Omaha Beach on D-Day, June 6, 1944.

an interim basis until June, when Richard Smith became the new executive director, a position he would hold for sixteen years.

Kenneth Levin became Beth El's seventeenth president in 1985. During the summer months that year, *Shabbat* services were held at the Ravinia Public School auditorium while asbestos materials were removed from the sanctuary building, an effort initiated by Dr. Edward Goldberg. Joseph Betensky, Vice President Administration, attended to all the arrangements. That summer the congregation also was introduced to Cantor Larry Josefovitz, who joined the congregation from the Park Synagogue in Cleveland, Ohio. He would serve at Beth El for the next two years. With the arrival of Cantor Josefovitz, the Ritual Committee unanimously made the decision to have the *shaliach tzibur* face toward the *aron kodesh*, the ark, during religious services, rather than toward the congregation, which had been the custom at Beth El up to that time. This was done in connection with the design of a new lectern and reading table for the Field Family Sanctuary.[122]

In the spring of 1986, Al Kopin announced that the Capital Fund and Endowment Campaign had received $2.8 million in gifts and pledges. Of that amount, more than $1 million would be held by the new North Suburban Synagogue Beth El Endowment Corporation to fund important educational programs of the congregation. The Endowment Corporation, under the stewardship of Richard Janger, would more than quadruple its assets over the next thirty years and continuously provide an important source of income to the synagogue. Also that year, in an effort to obtain the additional funds needed to undertake construction and still maintain fiscal responsibility with respect to the project, a loan of $1.3 million was negotiated with the First National Bank of Highland Park.

More changes occurred. At the urging of Rabbi Lebeau, *Siddur Sim Shalom*, newly published by the Rabbinical Assembly and the United Synagogue of America, was introduced,

---

122   This new arrangement was not met with universal approval. In a letter to former President Gerald Buckman, Harold Blumberg stated that he was "aghast" at the decision, which he felt "would bring us into the Orthodox view point...."

replacing the Silverman prayer book which had been in use since the earliest days of the synagogue. In June, 1986, Joni Mandel became the new Youth Community Director and Shifra Davis became the new director of the pre-school. That fall, the Field Family Sanctuary was literally lit up as the congregation's *Slichot* services preceding the High Holidays were televised around the country on the WGN-TV cable network. Commentary on the service was provided by Beth El's very own Rabbi Mordecai Simon, Executive Director of the Chicago Board of Rabbis.

By the end of 1986, after years of planning, construction of the new improvements finally commenced. On September 14, 1986, a formal groundbreaking ceremony was held for the new Posen Rabbinic and Administrative Wing, dedicated by the family of Faye Posen in memory of Sam Posen, longtime members of the congregation. Daily throughout the winter and spring of 1987 the work progressed, virtually every aspect of which was meticulously supervised by General William Levine, chairman of the House Committee.[123] The goal of the rabbi, to create the physical surroundings within which the synagogue could bring exciting and new educational programs to its children and its congregants, was near to realization. Many congregants joined in making major dedications to advance this effort, among them Benjamin and Bernice Cohen who, on December 14, 1986, dedicated the Religious School in memory of Jack and Mildred Cohen. In the summer of 1987, Rabbi Lebeau, with the approval of the Board, accepted on behalf of the synagogue the magnificent gift of twelve stained glass windows depicting the twelve tribes of Israel, created by artist Jerome Mann. Mann, his wife Lillian, and his sister and brother-in-law Rhoda Kreiter-Levine and General Levine, made the gift in memory of their parents. The windows were soon installed adjacent to the new main entryway into the renovated sanctuary.[124] In the fall of 1987,

---

123 General Levine, who at one time had been the highest-ranking Jewish officer in the United States Army, was granted special recognition for his efforts on behalf of the congregation at the annual meeting of the congregation in May, 1987.

124 As with the Azaz gates to the Kol Ami Museum, these windows were removed during the 2016 renovation work.

Irwin and Sharon Grossinger came forward to dedicate the newly constructed multi-purpose room as the Grossinger-Brickman Activity Center in memory of their parents. It soon became one of the most popular locations in the synagogue. And soon Milton and Iona Levenfeld would dedicate the synagogue's spacious *sukkah* as the Levenfeld Family Congregational *Sukkah*.

During the summer of 1987, due to the efforts of the Cantor Search Committee under the chairmanship of Jeffrey Wohlstadter, Henry Rosenblum of Congregation Oheb Shalom in South Orange, New Jersey, joined the congregation. Rejecting the English title of "cantor" in favor of the traditional Hebrew, Hazzan Rosenblum and his wife, Susan Ticker, and their young family, were warmly welcomed to the community. Hazzan Rosenblum first took the pulpit for *Shabbat* services on August 22, 1987.

Meanwhile, the congregation received a shock when Rabbi Lebeau, in the spring of 1987, announced that he had been called to serve as Vice-Chancellor of the Jewish Theological Seminary and reluctantly would be leaving the congregation for New York at the end of the year. The rabbi had decided he could not refuse the request of his longtime friend and colleague, Ismar Schorsch, Chancellor of the Seminary, to serve the entire Conservative movement in New York. In a letter dated May 5, 1987, President Levin informed the congregation of Rabbi Lebeau's departure, describing him as "a Rabbi who was sincerely interested in his fellow man....who would bring the entire staff to a high level of excellence, who would improve the school and youth program....and who was dignified, intelligent and personable....[O]f greater importance, he has been someone who each of us has been able to call 'friend'." Once again, the congregation would wonder about its future, and once again Eli Field would assure all that "the Torah would still be read" at Beth El. Promptly, a Rabbinic Search Committee was established jointly by President Levin and incoming President Howard Turner. Al Kopin was asked to be its chairman. On September 17, 1987, the committee unanimously recommended calling Rabbi Vernon H. Kurtz of Congregation Rodfei Zedek in Chicago to the pulpit and who, due to prior commitments, would officially assume his new duties at Beth El on August 1, 1988.

In November, 1987, over 500 congregants joined Sam and Deena Fraint for a farewell *Shabbat* luncheon in the Blumberg Auditorium. The assistant rabbi, who had served the congregation over the preceding four years, had accepted the call to serve as rabbi at Congregation Moriah in Deerfield. The following month, on December 6, the auditorium was again filled to capacity for a gala tribute dinner in honor of the Lebeaus. For nearly a decade Rabbi Lebeau had led the congregation to new heights of achievement and had provided the inspiration for its new dreams. He had helped heal the rifts in the congregation created a decade earlier and had been largely responsible for its growth in membership from approximately 750 families to over 1,100 families. With a mixture of sadness in his departure and pride in the recognition of his talents, the congregation bid farewell to Rabbi William and Beverly Lebeau.[125]

---

[125]   Rabbi Lebeau served as Vice-Chancellor of the Seminary and later also as dean of its rabbinical school until he stepped down in 2007. He continued to teach at the Seminary for a number of years before becoming a senior consultant to the Rabbinical Assembly.

V. THE SECOND GENERATION
(1987–1997)

The fall of 1987 through the spring of 1988 was a period of transition at Beth El. Rabbi Lebeau, although eager to assume his new responsibilities in New York, remained at Beth El until the end of December and made a commitment to return to officiate at bar and bat mitzvah celebrations through the following spring. Rabbi Kurtz honored his obligations to Rodfei Zedek through June, 1988 but made a concerted effort to attend Board meetings and to involve himself in major decisions at Beth El throughout that period. Despite some unavoidable problems, the transition went smoothly. Many individuals came forward to assist during the absence of rabbinic leadership. Rabbi Lawrence Charney, rabbi emeritus of Northwest Suburban Jewish Congregation in Morton Grove, Illinois, was retained by the congregation on a temporary basis to officiate at *Shabbat* services and at funerals. During periods when Rabbi Charney was unavailable, Rabbi Mordecai Simon was present to assist, as he had done on numerous occasions in the past. Also, Hazzan Rosenblum, along with Alan Weiner, were able to coordinate many of the religious programs and activities for the congregation during that period. Despite these unusual circumstances, Alan Miller, chairman of the Membership Committee, was able to announce in the spring of 1988 that membership in the congregation continued to rise.

Construction of the new facilities continued throughout this period. Soon, President Turner requested an increase of $700,000 in the construction budget and a corresponding increase in the mortgage loan. But as construction progressed, costs kept increasing, often for unanticipated items: additional asbestos materials had to be removed, portions of the parking lot required reconstruction, and the installation of additional health and safety measures were required by the Highland Park Fire Department. Also, as in past building campaigns, uncollected pledges posed a major problem. By March 1988, Michael Nadler, Treasurer, announced to the Board that despite the increased borrowings a major cash shortfall existed. Within two months, the amount of the mortgage was again increased. Total borrowings were now $2.2 million. Notwithstanding the looming financial emergency, the Board voted, over the strong objections of several past presidents, not to increase dues for the coming year.[126]

On April 24, 1988, the newly completed improvements were formally dedicated in a ceremony in the Field Family Sanctuary. Edith Kaye chaired the committee which organized that meaningful occasion. It was the fulfillment of a vision of a second generation at Beth El and it was a re-dedication not only of the congregation's physical facilities but also of its commitment to carry that vision into the future. Over 520 families had participated in the Capital Fund and Endowment Campaign and over $3 million had been raised. Although the formal Campaign ended with the completion of construction, the structure of the Campaign was designed to stay in place so that additional gifts could be made within an approved and organized framework. This farsighted plan proved to be very beneficial to the congregation as many additional gifts were made over the ensuing years.

Although without a full-time rabbi, many notable programs and staff changes occurred during this period.[127] In the fall of 1987, Barbara Spectre, formerly of Highland Park but since the 1960s a resident of Israel, visited Beth El as the United Synagogue Scholar.[128] Sandy Brown, Vice President Education,

---

[126] On April 28, 1988, during the Board discussion on the budget at that critical time, Rhoda Kreiter-Levine made a motion to save money by abolishing the professional choir for the High Holidays. A lengthy and emotional debate ensued, but the motion was withdrawn after Jeffrey Wohlstadter informed the Board that the choir was already under contract for the coming holidays!

[127] In the fall of 1987, Beth El lost one of its most devoted volunteers, Joseph Betensky. The following April the Board of Directors unanimously approved the dedication in his memory of the *tallit* and *tefilin* storage cabinet which he had designed by the entrance to the Sager Bet HaMidrash.

[128] See footnote 37. Barbara Spectre had married Rabbi Philip Spectre, who in 1967 was the founding rabbi of congregation Netzach Yisrael in Ashkelon, Israel, a "twin" congregation of Beth El. Rabbi Spectre later would serve as the Chief Rabbi of Sweden.

announced to the Board in December, 1987 that Cheryl Banks had been hired as the director of the Joseph and Mae Gray Cultural and Learning Center, a position she would hold with great effectiveness for the next twenty years. In June, 1988, Rabbi Peter Light, recommended by a search committee chaired by Larry Weiner, became the new assistant rabbi and Helene Moses became the new Youth Community Director. Perhaps the most heralded event of the year, however, was the 40th Anniversary Gala Celebration held on June 12, 1988. Planned by Herb Isaacs with the assistance of Ramona Choos and Jeffrey Wohlstadter, it was a huge success as over 600 people filled the Blumberg Auditorium to celebrate and enjoy an original musical production, "1988: Let's Celebrate," written by Roberta Caplan and Beth El's own Ed Shapiro, reviewing many of the highlights of Beth El's first forty years.

Rabbi Kurtz, his wife, Bryna, and their two daughters arrived at Beth El during the summer of 1988; he "officially" took the pulpit for the first time on August 27, 1988. Rabbi Kurtz and Bryna were both from Toronto, Ontario, Canada.[129] He had been ordained by the Jewish Theological Seminary in 1976 and in 1981 had received the degree of Doctor of Ministry from Chicago Theological Seminary. Shortly after arriving at Beth El, he shared a "State of the Synagogue Report" with the congregation. In it he set forth his concept of the three basic ideals uniting and making congregants feel at home at Beth El: a caring community, shared communal values, and shared institutional goals. Building on this, he looked forward to the challenge of creating a strong *kehila* at the synagogue which would serve to maintain Beth El "as a *Bet El*, a house of G-d." Rabbi Kurtz also believed that his service in providing leadership for community and professional organizations redounded to the benefit of the congregation in many ways. In keeping with that, in the fall of 1988 he became president of the Chicago Region of the Rabbinical Assembly and he continued to play an active role in Jewish Federation. Over the ensuing years he would continue to assume positions of high leadership in many local, national and

---

129   The Kurtzes both became American citizens in 1995.

international organizations.

With the arrival of Beth El's fifth senior rabbi, the congregation had a full schedule not only of its regular activities but also of many special events. In August, 1988, the Board, with the support of Rabbi Kurtz, approved the suggestion of Gail Winston to sponsor a forum at Beth El to discuss the controversial case of convicted spy Jonathan Pollard. On Wednesday evening, November 9, 1988, the congregation observed the fiftieth anniversary of Kristallnacht. That fall the Social Action Committee, under the chairmanship of Fran Levy, started the "Coats Against the Cold" program, which collected over 500 coats from congregants for needy people throughout the Chicago community. And on December 11, the congregation gathered in the Field Family Sanctuary for the formal installation ceremony of Rabbi Kurtz. Rabbi Kassel Abelson, president of the Rabbinical Assembly and senior rabbi of Congregation Beth El of Minneapolis, was the featured speaker.

In the fall of 1988, engraved bronze plaques recognizing the donors to the Capital Fund and Endowment Campaign were affixed to the marble wall in the sanctuary foyer. At the same time the Lucite plaques which had recognized donors in the 1960s Sanctuary Campaign were removed and replaced with new bronze plaques. (Similar recognition would be made for contributors to the Guaranteeing Our Future Campaign twelve years later.) These remain as a lasting tribute to the individuals who made possible the construction of a significant portion of the synagogue's facilities. Sadly, that fall Benjamin Harris passed away. The pioneer who is credited with creating the nucleus around which Beth El was founded remembered his synagogue to the end, leaving a bequest in his will to the Beth El Educational Endowment.

The first part of 1989 brought several noted scholars from Israel to speak at Beth El, including Rabbi Moshe Tutnauer, Dr. Marc Hirshman and Rabbi Shlomo Riskin. That spring, the Board of Directors authorized the creation of the Rabbi Philip L. Lipis Award to be granted in recognition of exceptional service to the congregation. Janet and Irving Robbin, who had served the synagogue for so many years and had endowed the annual Scholar in Residence program which bears their names, were the first recipients of that prestigious award on June 4, 1989 in an evening of tribute chaired by Len Birnbaum and Caryn Garber.[130]

In May, 1989, Morton Steinberg, son of Paul and Sylvia Steinberg, amongst the earliest families of Beth El, became the new president of the synagogue. For the first time, a member of Beth El's second generation had assumed that position of leadership in the congregation. The new administration was immediately faced with a financial crisis. Total loans for the recent construction had reached $2.35 million, including loans from the Sisterhood and $100,000 in emergency loans from individual congregants. The projected operational deficit for the year was $117,000 and in June the Board was informed that only $17,000 was on hand to pay salaries and other current expenses.[131] Quickly, daily cash reports were issued to the officers to keep them informed of the financial situation. Letters were sent out to members urgently requesting advance payment of future dues. Jack Frost, Financial Vice President, was appointed chairman of a Long Range Financial Planning Committee and by September a plan was adopted to concentrate on reducing the large debt. To do this, the building fund and other fees were increased and a special assessment (called "supplemental dues") of $330 per family ($160 for families who had been members less than five years) was imposed.[132] These steps proved successful and by the following spring the mortgage had been reduced by $300,000, the loans from Sisterhood and individual congregants had been repaid, and discussions were underway to restructure the remaining debt to save interest costs.

---

130 In subsequent years, this award was presented to Marge and Len Birnbaum, the Beth El Sisterhood and its past presidents, and Jack and Eenie Frost.

131 The location for meetings of the Board of Directors was now moved to the new Grossinger-Brickman Activity Center from the Zell Activity Room in the auditorium building. Before that, the meetings had been held in the living room of the mansion building.

132 An additional proposal to implement a raffle as a special fundraising event was defeated by the directors as being contrary to Beth El's tradition of not permitting gambling on the synagogue premises.

In addition to these measures, fundraising continued. One of the most significant gifts came from Myrna and Al Kopin, who in June 1989 dedicated the front garden of the synagogue as the Kopin Sallin Memorial Garden in memory of their parents. That site has continued as a location of beauty and tranquility literally surrounded on three sides by the activity of a vital and active synagogue community.[133]

The financial crisis did not slow the pace of activity at Beth El. One of Rabbi Kurtz's major goals was to develop a strong children's program at the congregation. As part of that program, Leann Buchman was hired as the new Youth Community Director in June 1989. In September, she reported to the Board on her plans for enhancing the Youth Community, which already included the Shalom Club for elementary school children, a Kadima group for junior high schoolers, and the USY group for high school students. Also that fall, the Tot Shabbat program, which had been operating successfully for several years, was expanded with the institution of the Mini-Minyan for older children. Eventually, this would be further expanded to include an active Junior Congregation. These three programs were very popular with parents of young children and were an important factor in attracting young families to the congregation. In the pre-school, new parent-toddler classes and infant programs were introduced under a special grant from the Board of Jewish Education, and a summer day camp for pre-school age children was reintroduced. Rabbi Kurtz also implemented innovative programs personally. In November, he began a monthly Lunch-in-the-Loop study group and in December he and Bryna led a group of congregants to Israel on the first of many such trips. He also began to teach the weekly Talmud study group at the synagogue which continues to meet.

---

[133] As part of the effort to raise funds for programs, Gene Siskel, the well-known movie critic, was instrumental in obtaining several significant grants to the Joseph and Mae Gray Cultural and Learning Center. Siskel had grown up in Glencoe and was an alumnus of Beth El's Hebrew School. He passed away in 1999 at the age of fifty-three. Many prominent individuals attended his funeral, held in the Field Family Sanctuary on February 22, 1999, including Roger Ebert, Mayor Richard M. Daley and Oprah Winfrey.

Over the years, Dorothy Wexler had worked hard to develop Beth El's Jack and Mildred Cohen Religious School into one of the best afternoon Hebrew schools in the country and in September, 1989, she was honored by the Chicago Board of Jewish Education (BJE) by being named "Educator of the Year." However, the Hebrew High School program, operated at the synagogue by the BJE, languished. Amy Pessis, Vice President Education, along with Ben Strauss, chairman of the High School Committee, worked with the BJE to try to rejuvenate the high school curriculum, but major changes would not be made until three years later.

1990 witnessed several changes in key personnel.[134] Alan and Linda Weiner and their family left Beth El in June after six years of devoted service. A special *kiddush* was held in their honor on Shavuot that spring. Also Rabbi Light, Janet and their family departed the community; he had accepted the position of rabbi at Congregation Beth Shalom in Memphis, Tennessee.[135] Jeffrey Abrams became the new ritual administrator and a search committee headed by Ernie Kaplan, Vice President Ritual, selected Jay David Sales to be the new assistant rabbi. But that summer also brought sadness to the congregation. In July, Harold Gorin, former president and *gabai hagadol* for religious services, passed away.[136] Just a few days later, Irving Robbin, a prominent figure not only in the synagogue but in all aspects of the Conservative movement, also died. At the August Board meeting, Al Kopin delivered a moving *d'var Torah* in memory of these two great men.

On November 4, 1990, another major dedication was made when the Beth El Pre-School was dedicated in memory of Paul S. and Sylvia Steinberg by their children, Morton and Miriam

---

134   1990 also brought a technological innovation to the congregation when in February Beth El acquired, from an anonymous donor, its first fax machine.

135   After fourteen years in Memphis, Rabbi Light moved to Marlborough, New Jersey, where, following a period of personal struggles, he suddenly passed away in 2008 at the age of forty-nine.

136   After Gorin, first Al Kopin and then Larry Weiner fulfilled the important role of *gabai hagadol* at weekly *Shabbat* services.

Steinberg and Joseph and Diane Steinberg. In the same month, due to the generosity of the Sisterhood and Harold and Ruby Blumberg, the Board approved the refurbishing of the Blumberg Auditorium under the direction of Mae Spitz. (The work was done during the summer of 1991, on time and under budget!) Also that fall, the Board approved expanding the location of the *yahrzeit* tablets into the memorial alcove beside the entry to the Sager Bet HaMidrash to meet the needs of the growing congregation, and Hazzan Rosenblum presented a memorable concert in the Field Family Sanctuary by a thirty-member group of Jewish teenagers from Riga, Latvia.

In January, 1991, the congregation shared a sense of concern with all Americans and Jews as the Persian Gulf War broke out in the Middle East and Israel came under missile attack from Iraq. Special security measures were taken at the synagogue, particularly at the school. An emergency meeting of the congregation was called by President Steinberg for February 4 to offer prayers and demonstrate support for the State of Israel. The Field Family Sanctuary was filled as Israeli Consul General Uri Bar Ner spoke of the situation in the Jewish state. That evening an amount in excess of $600,000 in Israel Bonds was raised, the largest amount from any congregation in the Midwest.

More changes occurred in the spring. The synagogue acquired a system to assist hearing-impaired congregants in participating more fully in worship services. It also commissioned artist Lorelei Gruss to create a specially designed *tzedakah* box of inlaid woods which was placed inside the entry to the Sager Bet HaMidrash.[137] Also that spring Rabbi Sales announced he was leaving the congregation[138] and a search committee, headed by Ernie Kaplan and Ted Levine, was appointed to identify a new assistant rabbi, but it would be almost two years before a replacement could be found. For the High Holidays in 1991 and again in 1992,

---

[137] The *tzedakah* box was stolen from the synagogue in the winter of 1998.

[138] After leaving Beth El, Rabbi Sales became a teacher at Jewish day schools in Washington, D.C. and then in Pittsburgh. He died at the young age of forty-one in 2004.

Rabbi Victor Hoffman was invited from Israel to lead the family services.[139]

Leonard Tenner became the new president of Beth El in May, 1991. By that time, the mortgage had been reduced to $1.6 million and the financial crisis had eased. Attention was directed to important issues of programming within the congregation, especially the educational program. In the fall of 1991, Fran Levy, Vice President Education, appointed a committee, chaired by Amy Pessis and Rabbi Charles Dobrusin, to study the feasibility of having the synagogue create its own high school of Hebrew studies. Within a few months, that committee, with the support of Rabbi Kurtz, concluded that the synagogue should take upon itself the responsibility of running a Hebrew High School starting in the fall of 1992. The Board quickly approved this recommendation. This was another milestone in the development of quality educational programming at Beth El. Randi Newman was soon named as the first administrator of the new high school and by January, 1993, 105 students, 90% of them children of members, were enrolled. In September, 1992, Miriam Sokol generously dedicated the new high school in memory of her husband and former synagogue president, Bernard S. Sokol.[140]

Other programming changes were also made. A committee chaired by Sally Stiefel addressed the issue of programming for senior citizens and soon the Over Fifty Group, later to be called the Sunday Afternoon Group, was formed and held its first program in October, 1991, featuring a visit by Rabbi Yechiel Eckstein. One of the more challenging and emotional changes in programming occurred in the spring of 1992 with respect

---

139 At about this time an unfortunate incident occurred at the Yom Kippur services in the Field Family Sanctuary, where all seats were "reserved" through the *musaf* service, but thereafter became "open" for the remainder of the day. While it was not unusual for some congregants to "save" some open seats for those coming from the high school service, on one Yom Kippur an older congregant refused to recognize the seats "saved" by a younger gentleman, resulting in probably the only actual fist fight to occur in the sanctuary.

140 The name of the Hebrew High School was modified to include the name of Miriam Sokol following her death in 2011.

to the establishment of the Bet HaMidrash Minyan. Several members of the congregation, informally headed by Michael ("Buzzy") and Mona Fishbane, had requested an alternate *minyan* which would provide a smaller, participatory service one *Shabbat* per month but otherwise would follow the same religious practices as the main service and would participate jointly in the congregational *kiddush*. When first proposed in March, 1992, this innovative concept was met with much skepticism and opposition, and in April almost the entire Board of Directors meeting, with special rules of procedure prepared by President Tenner, was devoted to a discussion of the merits of the proposal. Finally, the *minyan* was approved on a trial basis. It proved successful and has continued since that time.

In March, 1992, Rabbi Kurtz addressed a memo to the Board of Directors asking for the establishment of a "Task Force to work together with me on the issues that I raised concerning the high rate of intermarriage in the American Jewish community." While stating that he did not feel it was the task of the congregation to promote outreach for all people in the community, promoting educational opportunities for interfaith couples to learn the beauty and significance of Jewish life was important. As a direct outgrowth of that memo, the Joy of Judaism Intermarriage Task Force was established the following year under the leadership of Sam Shanes and Marc Siegel. Together, they put forth a structured program to address the concerns raised by Rabbi Kurtz.

Shifra Davis retired as Pre-School director in June, 1992. Mally Rutkoff headed the search committee which that summer brought Tammie Roth to Beth El as the new director of the Paul S. and Sylvia Steinberg Pre-School. Shortly thereafter, Karen Wolanka left Beth El to accept a position at Moriah Congregation. For many years Karen had served devotedly with Dorothy Wexler as the administrative secretary for the Cohen Religious School. In light of these changes and with the growth of both formal and informal educational programs at Beth El, a second Vice President Education position was created in the fall of 1992 and Sharon Goldenberg became the first person to hold that new office. Thereafter, the two vice presidents would annually divide between them the responsibilities in this critical area of synagogue life. Also in 1992 the Sisterhood, under co-presidents Helene Isaacs and Ruth Fischer, published *Tradition in the Kitchen II*. Like its predecessor, this cookbook was also a sellout.

By the fall of 1992, membership in the congregation exceeded 1,100 families despite the general economic recession of the early 1990s. The recession caused numerous instances of corporate "downsizing," resulting in many senior executives, many of whom resided on the North Shore, finding themselves unemployed. To deal with this crisis, several congregations in the Chicagoland area formed the Jewish Employment Network, which Beth El joined in the fall of 1992. Michael Nadler served as coordinator on behalf of the synagogue. And despite the economic hardships, Herb Isaacs, who for many years had been called upon to assist with the *Kol Nidre* appeal, reported that over $114,000 had been raised that Yom Kippur.

An important issue to which Rabbi Kurtz devoted his attention at this time was the issue of the role of women in the congregation's ritual practices. Since the days of Rabbi Dresner, women had participated in the Torah service and were counted for the purposes of constituting a *minyan*, but Beth El continued to follow the traditional interpretation of Jewish law which obligated men to serve as prayer leaders during religious services. Responding to an inquiry by Elena Silberman in 1992, the rabbi referred this matter to the Ritual Committee. Together, he and the committee members studied this issue and the *halacha* concerning it. As part of this process, two acknowledged scholars in this area, Professors Joel Roth and Judith Hauptman, both of the Jewish Theological Seminary, presented a discourse on this subject to the congregation on May 22, 1994.

At a meeting of the Ritual Committee on October 24, 1994, Rabbi Kurtz presented his reasoned responsum entitled "Women Prayer Leaders." In it, he reached the conclusion that "for a woman to lead the congregation in public prayer beyond *kabbalat Shabbat* and *pesukei d'zimra*, she herself must be obligated for those prayers. Thus, women who accept the obligation of daily prayer at its specific time,.... [by signing] a document to testify to her willingness to accept this new status...., will be allowed to lead the congregation in prayer." Although recognizing that his opinion would not satisfy everyone, Rabbi Kurtz hoped that his decision would be accepted as being loyal to *halachic* tradition. The rabbi's decision was met with mixed responses. A few families, totally opposed to this new policy, resigned from the congregation and left the community. Others met informally to voice their opposition to what they believed was not a *halachically* correct interpretation. However, only a handful of women actually undertook to assume the status described in the rabbi's opinion and in practice very little changed. And it was not until the *musaf* service on *Shabbat* morning August 16, 1997, that Fortunee Belilos became the first woman to lead a religious service at Beth El.[141]

Ernest Kaplan became president of Beth El in May, 1993, and he continued the effort to collect outstanding accounts receivable and to reduce the mortgage debt. One effort was to amend the by-laws to permit the suspension of members who had been in arrears in their financial obligations for significant periods of time. In addition, a new display board to acknowledge the generosity and leadership of participants in the Fair Share Dues program was designed for the sanctuary foyer. These efforts were successful and by March, 1994, Robert Weber, Treasurer, reported that the balance of the synagogue's mortgage had been reduced to $1.3 million. Of course, the unexpected still occurred: a fire in the boiler room in the mansion building in August caused over $60,000 in damage. Fortunately, it was fully covered by insurance.

In May, 1993, Miriam Steinberg, on behalf of the Ritual Committee, presented to the directors a "Position Paper on Bar/Bat Mitzvah Celebrations" which addressed the "conspicuous consumption," "excessive expenditures," "inappropriate celebrations," and "displays of disrespect" which characterized

---

[141]   A congregant for several years, Belilos eventually left Highland Park to attend the H.L. Miller Cantorial School at the Jewish Theological Seminary.

many aspects of what should be an important life-cycle religious ceremony. The document had been prepared by the North Shore Intercongregational Task Force comprised of fourteen Conservative and Reform congregations in which she and Alan Miller had represented Beth El. With the support of Rabbi Kurtz, the paper was accepted by the Board.

A new Beth El tradition grew out of neighborhood friendships beginning in the spring of 1993. Following religious services on the first day of the holiday of Shavuot, David Shapiro and his wife Lori Stark and their neighbors Mark and Babette Daskin invited a few friends from their neighborhood to a backyard picnic. Over the next few years, this Shavuot gathering expanded to include numerous families from the congregation and by 2014 the Shapiros hosted the Beth El Congregational Shavuot Picnic at their home on Sheridan Road. This annual event has since been hosted at the synagogue.

The two-year wait for a new assistant rabbi ended in the summer of 1993 when Rabbi Jay Stein and his wife Melissa moved to the community. They were warmly welcomed by the congregation and quickly became involved in synagogue activities. That fall, in the absence of William Weisel, Gadi Fishman served as cantor for the High Holiday family service.

The Ritual Committee under Vice President Ritual Robert Berger considered several new ideas during 1993. First, in response to a request from several congregants, it implemented an abbreviated monthly late Friday night service for families with young children. Also, the Ritual Committee raised with Rabbi Kurtz the question of whether or not *birkat kohanim*, or *duchanen*, the traditional blessings performed by the *kohanim* of the congregation, was appropriate at Beth El. Rabbi Kurtz, after studying the issue carefully, decided that this was *halachically* proper for Festivals and the High Holidays and the practice was instituted at Beth El during Shavuot services in the spring of 1994.[142]

---

142   In another matter, the Ritual Committee voted to eliminate the annual *Kol Nidre* Torah procession of the trustees, which had been a tradition at Beth El since the earliest days of the congregation. This attempt failed when the trustees loudly protested the proposed change.

Rabbi Kurtz took another step to implement his program focusing on children when in September, 1993, he outlined a plan to develop a "parenting center" at Beth El. Soon, "Lamazel" classes for expectant couples were scheduled. The following fall a new Sunday morning parenting program for fathers and their young children called "Daddies and Darlings" was instituted by the Steinberg Pre-School. Within one month enrollment in the program doubled and a waiting list existed.

At the United Synagogue Convention in November, 1993, Beth El was awarded two Solomon Schechter awards: one for achievements by the Gray Cultural and Learning Center and one in recognition of the *Vav* class parent-child program implemented by Rabbi Lebeau and enriched by Rabbi Kurtz. In February of the following year, the Social Action Committee began an important new program when Renee Bearak, its chairwoman, announced the congregation's participation in the Yad L'Yad program in conjunction with Chicago Action for Soviet Jewry. The congregation was paired with the Jewish community of Berdichev, Ukraine in the former Soviet Union in a partnership which over the years would bring much satisfaction and pleasure to Beth El's congregants and many benefits to the residents of Berdichev. In June, 1994, David Solomon, Vice President Finance, introduced a new concept for the congregation's annual fundraiser. Called "Weigh the Possibilities," it was an auction of donated merchandise and kosher delicacies. The highlight of the successful evening was a live auction conducted by auctioneer extraordinaire Jerry Blumberg.

Rabbi Kurtz, in addition to his duties at the synagogue and his leadership roles in many local and national organizations, began serving as a rotating rabbinic columnist for the *Chicago Jewish News* in the fall of 1994. He also organized a congregational trip to visit the new United States Holocaust Memorial in Washington, D.C.; it was a huge success and quickly sold out. Sadly, in December of that year, past president Albert Kopin died at the young age of fifty-nine. A true pillar of the congregation and of the Conservative movement, he was fondly memorialized at a Board of Directors meeting. Three years later, Myrna and other members of the Kopin family generously dedicated the portico entry into the sanctuary building in his memory.

In the spring of 1995, Leann Buchman Blue, who had served as Youth Community Director for six years, announced she would be leaving Beth El. Quickly, Donald Horwitz, chairman of the Youth Committee, headed a search committee which hired Michael Gluck to serve in that position. At the same time, the Board of Directors, in an extraordinary move, voted "a one-time exception" to the general policy limiting the term of an assistant rabbi to a total of three years, thus enabling Rabbi Stein, who had been so effective in all of his endeavors at the synagogue, especially in engaging young families to become active within the congregation, to extend his stay at Beth El. Throughout this period, Michael Sadoff, with assistance from Daniel Hoseman, chaired the Personnel Committee of the congregation and, with little recognition of their important work, made a tremendous contribution in reviewing, evaluating and negotiating contracts with almost every member of the professional staff.

In May, 1995, Richard Janger, the new president of the synagogue, presented the concept of leadership development as a major theme of his administration. This was an effort to produce qualified leaders for the synagogue in the years ahead. A Mission Statement for the congregation prepared by the Leadership Development Committee was introduced to the Board by Jeff Kopin, its chairman. It was approved and subsequently incorporated into the by-laws of the congregation. The Beth El Mission Statement reads as follows:

> We are a congregation of families and individuals who come together to pray, to study, and to create a warm and welcoming community. We seek to preserve and enhance our People's traditions within the context of Conservative Judaism. We aspire to strengthen our Jewish identity to meet the challenges of a changing environment. We endeavor to provide resources to help us relate to God, understand the ways of God and enrich the Jewish con-

tent of our lives. We encourage our members to serve worthwhile causes within our Congregation and the wider Jewish and world communities. We are committed to support Israel. We educate our children so they commit to the cultural, spiritual, and ethical values of our People.

Throughout the next two years, workshops and seminars on leadership development were presented, including a Participation Fair for the entire congregation. Also in 1995, Manny Marczak announced that for the first time in thirty-five years, the Men's Club had received the Torch Award from the National Federation of Jewish Men's Club for best overall activities.

In November, 1995, the congregation joined the rest of the Jewish people in expressing shock and condolences following the assassination of Israeli Prime Minister Yitzchak Rabin and special recognition was made by the Board of the need for Jewish unity and peace throughout the world. The following spring, the late Prime Minister's daughter, Dalia Rabin-Pelossof, spoke to the congregation at the annual Jewish United Fund dinner.

1996 saw several more changes at the synagogue. In February, Mally Rutkoff, Vice President Administration, implemented a new format for the synagogue bulletin,[143] and the Board of Directors thanked June Frydman for serving as editor for the previous 110 consecutive editions of the bulletin.[144] That spring, Jack Blumberg, Vice President Ritual,[145] announced that a new sound system for the Field Family Sanctuary would be installed by June. Also, the congregation granted Rabbi Kurtz a three-month sabbatical; the rabbi utilized that time during the fall

---

[143] The new monthly bulletin would have as many as sixteen pages filled with announcements, photographs, short articles, a column by the rabbi, acknowledgments of gifts, and notices of the numerous programs constantly being presented by the synagogue and its auxiliaries.

[144] Shortly after this, due to the efforts of Cheryl Banks and Rabbi Stein, Beth El established its own webpage on the Internet. It also acquired its official e-mail address: nssbe@nslsilus.org, which was later changed to nssbe@ nssbethel.org.

[145] Blumberg, a resident of Highland Park, had previously lived in Waukegan and had served as president of Beth El's neighbor to the north, Congregation Am Echod.

of 1996 and spring of 1997 to make important visits to Jewish communities in many parts of the world, including Cuba, Tunisia, and Israel, returning with fascinating reports on these trips. In the summer of 1996, Mark Stadler, originally hired to lead the Junior Congregation, became the new ritual director when Jeff Abrams left Beth El to take a position in Portland, Oregon. And that fall Katie Ostrander, who had loyally worked as secretary to Dick Smith and had been a friend to all congregants, retired from Beth El after ten years of devoted service.

Soon the congregation was reminded once again that things always change. In the winter of 1997, Dorothy Wexler, the extraordinary educational director of Beth El since 1981, announced she would be retiring in June, 1998. She was honored by the congregation at a special *kiddush* the following May. Quickly, Rabbi Kurtz prepared "Beth El Education: 1998 and Beyond," outlining recommendations for enhancing the overall educational program at Beth El, pointing out that Beth El "should be seen as a congregation of learners who support educational enterprises in all of their endeavors." Shortly thereafter, Sandy Brown was appointed to chair the Educational Structure Task Force to evaluate, together with Rabbi Kurtz, the congregation's educational programs to prepare for a new director for that important aspect of the synagogue. A few weeks later, Hazzan Rosenblum notified the congregation that he had accepted the position of dean of the H. L. Miller Cantorial School at the Jewish Theological Seminary, and he also would be leaving Beth El and moving to New York in June, 1998.

In May, 1997, Gerald Blumberg became Beth El's twenty-third president, forty-seven years after his father had been installed as Beth El's second president. That summer Karen Kopin, Vice President Education, announced with great pride that the Paul S. and Sylvia Steinberg Pre-School had been granted full accreditation by the National Academy of Early Childhood Programs. In November, Karen Kesner, also a Vice President Education, informed the directors that with close to 700 children enrolled in the various congregational schools, adequate space was becoming a critical issue. The directors promptly authorized the

Board of Education to undertake immediately "a review of the future space needs for the schools with the objective of developing a long-term plan for classroom and other space needs." It had the ring of history, an echo of Beth El's past.

VI. TRADITION AND CHANGE – THE NEW MILLENNIUM (1997–2008)

With the pending changes in important professional positions at the synagogue announced in 1997, search committees were appointed to seek qualified replacements: Karen Bieber chaired the search for a new educational director, Jack Blumberg was asked to serve as chairman of the Hazzan Search Committee, and Jeff Kopin headed the search for a new assistant rabbi.[146] By the summer of 1998, Hazzan Larry Goller of Congregation B'nai Israel in Millburn, New Jersey, had accepted the invitation to serve at Beth El. He first led *Shabbat* services on August 1, 1998. Also that summer, Aaron Klein, educational director of Northwest Suburban Jewish Congregation in Morton Grove, joined Beth El as its new educational director. Finding an acceptable assistant rabbi proved more difficult, and when the search committee reported that it could not recommend a candidate for that position, the congregation engaged its own Rabbi Mordecai Simon to serve as Rabbinic Associate for the coming year.

Since the fall of 1996, plans were being developed for a year-long celebration of Beth El's 50th anniversary, an occasion Rabbi Kurtz described as "a time to celebrate the past, solidify the present and guarantee the future." Helene Isaacs, Fran Levy and Ted Banks were appointed co-chairs of the 50th Anniversary Celebration and, together with Rabbi Kurtz, began to plan a series of special events for the synagogue's jubilee. One of the first would be a visit by Rabbi Joseph Telushkin as the Robbin Scholar-in-Residence in November, 1997. He was followed by other distinguished speakers, including Dennis Prager at the annual JUF dinner in April and Dr. Jack Wertheimer, Provost of the Jewish Theological Seminary, who delivered the annual Amy

---

[146] Rabbi Stein, who left Beth El in 1998 after five successful years, eventually became the senior rabbi at Har Zion Temple in suburban Philadelphia in 2004.

and Irving Frankel Memorial Lecture later that month and who was accompanied by Rabbi William Lebeau. The congregation's former rabbi, who maintained close and cordial friendships with the synagogue's members and professional staff, had become dean of the Rabbinical School at the Seminary in addition to his duties as Vice-Chancellor. Also that spring, Angie Levenstein, daughter of Harold and Ruby Blumberg, chaired a committee which undertook extensive videotaping as an archival record of many of the people who were part of the Beth El story. In addition, initial plans were formulated for a special $6 million fundraising campaign which was intended to retire the remaining outstanding indebtedness of the congregation. In line with Rabbi Kurtz's [147] vision, it was designated the "Guaranteeing Our Future Capital Campaign" and it would prove to be very successful. The festive formal celebration of the 50th anniversary, "An Affair to Remember," was held in the Blumberg Auditorium on May 24, 1998. A highlight of the evening was the presentation of the Rabbi Philip L. Lipis Award to the three remaining founders of the congregation, Mae Gray and Harold and Ruby Blumberg.

Following the festivities surrounding the 50th anniversary celebration, the congregation turned its attention to more immediate and practical needs. Richard Smith reported on projects to upgrade the Grossinger-Brickman Activity Center, seal the parking lot, renovate certain classrooms, and upgrade the synagogue's computer system. In the fall, the congregation purchased the home at 1380 Lincoln Avenue South for use by Hazzan Goller and his family. Also, Sandy Starkman, who over the next several years would become a leader of adult educational programming at Beth El, announced that a Florence Melton Adult Mini-School,[148] a project of the Hebrew University in Jerusalem, would open on the North Shore in January, 1999. It would provide many opportunities for serious adult

[147] In June of 1998, Rabbi Kurtz was the recipient of the Rabbi Simon Greenberg Rabbinic Achievement Award at the annual Chicago dinner of the Jewish Theological Seminary.

[148] The North American director of the Melton Schools from 1989 through 2008 was Beth El's own Dr. Betsy Dolgin Katz.

education and continues today.[149] Sadly, on January 3, 1999, Harold Blumberg, who had so passionately supported and helped build Beth El for over half a century, passed away at the age of eighty-eight. His funeral was held at the synagogue and Morton Steinberg presented a fitting tribute to "Mr. Beth El" at the Board of Directors meeting later that month.

For many years, the number of volunteer Torah readers had been diminishing in the congregation. Determined to remedy this, past president Howard Turner, in the spring of 1999, outlined his proposal for a program to encourage congregants of all ages to chant the Torah and participate in *Shabbat* services. It was called the Ba'al Korei Institute, and it was enthusiastically approved by the Board of Directors. The Ba'al Korei Institute would soon have over 100 members, each of whom had served as a Torah reader at least twice in one year; an annual member dinner would be a highlight of the program. Also that spring, Robert Ferencz, Vice President Ritual, announced that Rabbi David Lerner had accepted an offer to become the assistant rabbi of Beth El beginning in the summer of 1999. A reception honoring the new rabbi and his wife Sharon was held in conjunction with *Slichot* services in the fall.

Alan Rutkoff became Beth El's new president in May, 1999, and soon events outside of Highland Park, specifically a shooting attack on Jewish residents in West Rogers Park in Chicago and at a Jewish school in Los Angeles, prompted him to express his concern for safety at Beth El. Consultations were held with law enforcement agencies and the Board authorized Rutkoff to act to enhance the security at the synagogue. Soon a uniformed security guard was hired, a security system with a camera and a buzzer system at the front entry was installed, and increased Highland Park Police Department patrols were instituted.

The "public" phase of the Guaranteeing Our Future Capital Campaign was unveiled at Rosh Hashanah services in the fall of 1999. Len Birnbaum, as he had done so often in the past,

---

149 Things appeared to be going so smoothly at the congregation at that time that the minutes of the Board meeting on December 17, 1998 reflected that the meeting was called to order at 8:10 pm and, after all business had been addressed, was adjourned at 8:40 pm – a record for a Board meeting.

designed a special brochure for the Campaign. By that time, due to the efforts of the Campaign leadership, particularly Richard Janger, Chuck Kafenshtok and Scott Heyman, $4.5 million had already been pledged to the Campaign and Pearl Kagan, Treasurer, was able to announce that the congregation's debt had been reduced to $800,000. By the following fall, when the congregation celebrated the conclusion of the Campaign, 582 families had participated, contributing over $6.5 million in only three years. The Campaign had also increased the assets of the Endowment Corporation to over $2 million and the synagogue's debt had been further reduced, with a significant reserve established for future contingencies. It had been the most successful fundraising effort in the history of the synagogue.

Rabbi Lerner's presence at Beth El began to be felt shortly after his arrival. He soon began a very successful *perek yomi* study program, which would continue for the next three years. That would be followed by a series of classes and sessions on spirituality in Jewish life, beginning with a Spiritual Walk in the Botanic Gardens in Glencoe. Later, Rabbi Lerner organized a spiritual *Shabbat*, a *kabbalistic* yoga class, and other programs which attracted the participation of many congregants. To mark the beginning of the new millennium, which would occur on Friday night, December 31, 1999, Rabbi Lerner organized "*Shabbat* of the Century." Over 200 people attended *kabbalat Shabbat* services that evening followed by a joyous congregational dinner.

A very special event in the history of the synagogue, and in the career of its rabbi, occurred in March, 2000 when Rabbi Kurtz was installed as the president of the international Rabbinical Assembly. At the installation ceremonies held at Har Zion Temple in Philadelphia, President Rutkoff delivered a most memorable address. Over forty members of Beth El were in attendance that evening and Rabbi Kurtz viewed the occasion as one of the highlights of his professional career. For the ensuing two years, the special Rabbinical Assembly Torah mantel adorned a Torah scroll in the Field Family Sanctuary.

In April, 2000, Michael Gluck, who had been so successful

as Youth Community Director during the previous five years, announced he would be leaving Beth El. Over 220 Beth El children were active in USY, Kadima and Shalom Club (and a Beth El USYer, Shira Steinberg, had been elected USY Midwest Regional President). Soon, Lynn Cohen, Vice President Education, headed a search committee for a new youth director, and William Planer was hired to serve as Director of Youth Community and Informal Programs, a position intended to promote informal family activities as well as youth programming. That summer, Karen Kesner, Vice President Administration, hired a new head custodian, Costica Mihailescu, who would loyally serve the congregation for the next seventeen years. She also oversaw the installation of a handicapped lift for access to the Sager Bet HaMidrash as well as the construction of a portable wheelchair ramp to provide access to the *bimah* in the Field Family Sanctuary.

Events were happening in the Chicago Jewish community in which Beth El members played important roles. The General Assembly of the Jewish Federations of North America was held in Chicago in the fall of 2000, in which many present and future leaders of the synagogue participated, a reflection of the growing overlap of individuals with close ties to Federation holding leadership roles at Beth El. Also that fall, the newly established Chicagoland Jewish High School, affiliated with the Solomon Schechter Day Schools, held its first classes in Morton Grove, another venture with many of the Beth El community in key leadership positions.

By the winter of 2001, the synagogue had purchased the home at 930 Judson Avenue for Hazzan Goller and his growing family and had sold the house on Lincoln Avenue South. Also, William Planer left Beth El to pursue a new opportunity in his hometown of Atlanta and Michael Gluck, along with his wife Rachel, returned to lead the Youth Community on an interim basis. (Rachel would continue to serve as adviser for the Kadima program until the summer of 2009.) In addition, Harriet Ost was hired to serve as the part-time director of adult education at the synagogue.

In April, 2001, making a distinct change in precedent at the synagogue, the Board of Directors voted to extend a commitment to retain Rabbi Kurtz as the rabbi of the congregation through 2019. Rabbi Kurtz had developed close bonds with the Beth El community and had provided effective leadership to the dynamic congregation during his first thirteen years at Beth El. The rabbi viewed his professional responsibilities as extending not only to congregants but also to major Jewish organizations beyond the community. In addition to serving as president of the Rabbinical Assembly, he was a member of the Conference of Presidents of Major Jewish Organizations, had served as president of the Chicago Board of Rabbis, and had been vice chairman of the Jewish Federation of Metropolitan Chicago. Soon he would serve as president of MERCAZ USA and MERCAZ Olami and as a member of the Board of Governors of the Jewish Agency for Israel. This involvement inured to the benefit of the congregation, spreading the achievements and accomplishments of the synagogue throughout the Conservative Jewish world and making Beth El a "known quantity" as a leader in Jewish life and learning.[150] Through the efforts of the rabbi, renowned speakers and scholars were welcomed at the synagogue to enrich the lives of its congregants. Among the notable individuals to appear that year were Rabbi Elliot Dorff, Rector of the University of Judaism, Rabbi Matthew Futterman, president of the Rabbinical Assembly of Israel, and Dr. Burton Visotsky, professor of Midrash at the Jewish Theological Seminary. The rabbi's activities also reflected the involvement of the synagogue's membership in senior leadership positions in local, national and international organizations dedicated to benefiting Israel and the Jewish people.[151]

150   In the fall of 2001, Rabbi Kurtz was honored to attend the annual White House Hanukkah reception at the invitation of President and Mrs. Bush.

151   These organizations included the U.S. Holocaust Memorial Museum, Jewish Federation of Metropolitan Chicago, Magen David Adom, Jewish National Fund, Chicagoland Jewish High School, Camp Ramah in Wisconsin, Solomon Schechter Day Schools, and Israel Bonds. In 2006, Beth El members held an unprecedented three of the fifteen seats on the Leadership Council of Conservative Judaism (Vernon Kurtz, president of MERCAZ USA; Alan H. Silberman, president of Masorti Olami; and Morton Steinberg, president of the National Ramah Commission) and three were members of the Board of Governors of the Jewish Agency (Kurtz, Silberman and Richard Wexler).

On June 10, 2001, another historic first occurred at Beth El: Karen Kesner became the first woman to serve as president of the congregation, a position well earned by her years of hard work and effective leadership.[152] At the same time, Dick Smith retired after sixteen years as executive director and Ken Levin, a former Beth El president, was retained to fill that position upon the recommendation of a search committee chaired by Mally Rutkoff.

The al-Qaeda terror attacks in New York and Washington, D.C. on September 11, 2001 stunned the Beth El community as they did all Americans. Special services were convened at the synagogue to memorialize those lost in the attacks and to offer prayers for the injured. As a symbol of the continued devotion of the congregation to the United States and Israel, flags of both countries were thereafter displayed with pride on the *bimah* in the Field Family Sanctuary.[153] Yet life at Beth El went on, although with a greater concern for the physical security of the synagogue and its members. President Kesner appointed a Long Range Planning Committee to map out strategies for Beth El's continued growth. Jennifer Bearman, from Minneapolis, became the new youth director, and the congregation retired the Hertz *chumashim* that had been in use since its earliest days, replacing them with *Etz Chayim chumashim*, newly published by the Rabbinical Assembly and United Synagogue. In the spring of 2002, through the generosity of Ellen and Arnold Rissman, the extensive collection of ritual, historic and cultural artifacts held by the Kol Ami Museum, many originally from the Spertus family, was formally dedicated as the Arnold Rissman Family Kol Ami Museum.[154]

---

[152] After her term as president, Kesner continued to serve the congregation in the important role of chairman of the Gift Committee, a low-profile position but one in which she excelled. She continues in that position to the present.

[153] Interestingly, the Men's Club annual blood drive that fall was cancelled due to the over-supply of donations following the events of 9/11.

[154] The name of the museum was changed in 2017 to the Rissman Kol Ami Collection.

The United States was not the only country affected by acts of terrorism in the new millennium. In 2001, Israel began suffering from the events of the Second Intifada, Palestinian terrorist attacks on civilian targets throughout the country. Soon, tourism to Israel almost ceased, and the economy of the country quickly felt the impact of those events. The following year, Rabbi Kurtz voiced his concern that the number of young people visiting and studying in Israel was so low that it could impact that generation's connection to Israel. Efforts were made to encourage visits to the Jewish state and in the fall of 2002 a community-wide Shop For Israel Fair, which brought hundreds of merchants from Israel to this country, was held at North Shore Congregation Israel. Thousands of people attended the highly successful event, and over eighty members of Beth El volunteered to work at the fair.

At the May, 2002 meeting of the Board of Directors, Seth Pines, on behalf of the House Committee, reported that the almost forty-year-old heating and air conditioning system servicing the Blumberg Auditorium and Field Family Sanctuary was "on the verge of a meltdown" and needed to be replaced immediately. This was a major project, eventually costing in excess of $1.2 million. While the synagogue utilized a portion of its reserves for this project, additional borrowing was needed and a new mortgage was obtained at the Northern Trust Company in Chicago. By that fall, the new rooftop HVAC units had been delivered (by helicopter) and installed. The expensive new system was expected to last another forty years.

By this time, concern was growing over the reduced pace of new members joining the synagogue. At the suggestion of the Membership Committee, the dues structure was revised into just three categories, based on age, and membership continued to increase, albeit at a slower pace. By the fall of 2002, Beth El's membership had risen to an all-time high of 1,130 families and Jill Bernstein, Vice President Education, reported that enrollment in the schools remained vigorous, with 450 students in the Cohen Religious School and 193 children enrolled in the Steinberg Pre-School. In addition, over 100 Beth El children were attending the Solomon Schechter Day School and three were students at the new Chicagoland Jewish High School.

Larry and Enid Arnowitz became co-chairs of the Social Action Committee in the fall of 2002. Over the next several years, they would invigorate and develop innovative programming for that important aspect of the congregation. This included "twinning" with Congregation Comunidad Dor Jadash in Buenos Aires, Argentina, similar to Beth El's special relationships with the Masorti congregations in Ashkelon, Israel and Berdichev, Urkraine. (Rueben Saferstein, rabbi of the Dor Jadash, would visit Beth El and speak to the congregation in the spring of 2004.) The following May, the Social Action Committee participated in a Walk to End Homelessness at B'nai Tikvah Congregation in Deerfield, and it annually sponsored food drives at Thanksgiving and coat drives to benefit local charities.

In January, 2003, Eli and Dina Field, whose grandson, Matthew, was a student in the Rabbinical School of the Jewish Theological Seminary, endowed a chair in Jewish history at the Seminary. Dr. Benjamin Gampel, who would hold that chair, came to Beth El to honor the Field family.[155] That spring, the Seminary also conferred an Honorary Doctor of Divinity degree on Rabbi Kurtz on the occasion of the 25th anniversary of his rabbinic ordination.

The efforts of Cheryl Banks, director of the Gray Cultural and Learning Center, were recognized in 2003 by the Association of Jewish Libraries, which awarded her the Fannie Goldstein Award for her ongoing contribution to the profession of Judaica librarianship. Since 1988, Banks had built the Cultural and Learning Center into the largest synagogue library in the Midwest, with over 25,000 titles and hundreds of audio and video tapes and CDs. Over the next several years, she would oversee major improvements to the Cultural and Learning Center, including extensive renovations, first to the Maxwell Abbell Library and then to the central core of the Learning Center, dedicated as the Bernard and Edith Kaye Reading Room in 2006.

---

[155] Eli and Dina Field, whose commitment and devotion to Beth El had continued unabated for more than fifty years, both passed away in 2006.

Financially and programmatically, the synagogue reached new heights by the fall of 2003. Pearl Kagan, who had become the president of the congregation in May, was able to refinance the outstanding mortgage debt at a lower rate of interest, saving the congregation approximately $56,000 annually in interest payments. Lynn Schrayer, Vice President Finance, reported total collections of $252,000 in the Fair Share Dues program and from the *Kol Nidre* Appeal, and Jay Levine, Treasurer, assured the Board that the synagogue was in "excellent financial condition." In fact, the financial statements from that period showed a surplus of $95,000. In the area of education, 175 students were enrolled in the Bernard H. Sokol Hebrew High School, an all-time high according to Bunny Tier, Vice President Education, and over 300 young people were participating in the Youth Community Program. The B.E.A.N.S. (Beth El at North Suburban) USY group was the largest chapter in the Midwest Region of United Synagogue and had been selected as Chapter of the Year the previous spring. When Jennifer Bearman regrettably decided to return to Minneapolis, a search committee chaired by Gary Goldman quickly recommended bringing Aliza Schlamowitz to Beth El as the new youth director in the summer of 2003. And Rosh Hashanah in the fall of 2003 saw a new family service organized and run by Fran Sherman, designed for five-and-six-year-old children and their parents. It was held in the Grossinger-Brickman Activity Center and with seventy families in attendance, it was a "standing room only" event.

Hazzan Goller's programmatic efforts were also notable. In 2003, he formed the Cantor's Club to teach high school students *davening* skills and also convened similar classes for adults. He also worked extensively with the Ba'al Korei Institute, which was awarded a Gold Solomon Schechter Award at the annual convention of United Synagogue of Conservative Judaism in October. He arranged for the appearance at Beth El of the well-known Israeli singer Shuli Natan in April, 2003, and the annual Spring Music Festival, produced by the hazzan and the Men's Club and featuring the Beth El Youth Chorale, was always a popular program. The hazzan was also chosen that fall to serve as president of the Midwest Region Cantor's Assembly and the following January, he and Karen Kesner organized a very successful and well attended benefit concert at Beth El for that organization: "From the Bimah to Broadway to the Borsht Belt."[156]

Throughout this period, the annual rhythm of the synagogue began with High Holiday services in the fall and usually culminated with the annual congregational fundraiser (what many on the Executive Committee and Board of Directors began to call the "Big Event") in the spring, which was followed by summer religious services led by congregants and organized annually by Larry Goldstein. The congregation and its affiliates functioned smoothly,[157] serving an important role in the lives of the members and their children and dealing with new or unexpected matters as they arose. As always, raising funds to maintain and enhance the facilities and programs was a constant challenge, regularly met by the generosity of the membership.

In the spring of 2004, a new congregational website was implemented with major input from Cheryl Banks. Realizing the importance of the Internet, the synagogue soon began sending emails containing condolence notices and announcements of weekly events, a practice well received by the congregation. Also that spring, Rabbi Lerner announced he had been called to serve as rabbi of Temple Emunah in Lexington, Massachusetts. Rabbi Lerner had introduced many innovative programs and developed close friendships with many congregants, especially young members. There was no doubt that he would be missed. Soon, a search committee headed by Jeff Kopin recommended bringing Michael Schwab to Beth El to fill the position of assistant rabbi. Rabbi Schwab and his wife Erica moved into the synagogue's condominium townhouse on Judson Avenue in August,

---

156   Rod Slutsky, congregational secretary, noted in the minutes that for this event, the fundraising was "low key (no pun intended)."

157   In the fall of 2003, the Sisterhood announced it would not have one president, but a Presidential Committee of five women, each to serve as president for a two-month term. The five were Gabrielle Rousso, Ruth Fischer, Marilyn Lewis, Elise Frost and Susan Saper. This arrangement was not long-lasting, although subsequently the Sisterhood occasionally elected co-presidents.

2004 and were warmly welcomed by the congregation.

An issue of concern to the congregation's leadership for some time was appropriate dress and behavior for families of bar and bat mitzah celebrants. Well over seventy-five *b'nai mitzvah* were scheduled annually and many families were unaware of the standards of modesty and respectfulness at Beth El. The Ritual Committee, under the leadership of Michael Rosenberg, Vice President Ritual, had undertaken to compile these standards in written format and in August, 2004 it published "Guidelines on Appropriate Dress at the Synagogue for Bar/Bat Mitzvah," a well written guide to synagogue etiquette and values and a valuable outline for proper conduct at religious services. Also, the Ritual Committee, recognizing the *Intifada* erupting in Israel and the engagement of American forces in wars in Iraq and Afghanistan, inserted special prayers for the U. S. Armed Forces and Israel Defense Forces in all the synagogue's *siddurim*.

By the fall of 2004, membership growth had again slowed and was characterized as "flat" by the Membership Committee. Efforts were made to address this potentially serious issue, including more frequent personal contacts with new and potential members, sending *Shabbat* baskets to new members, and scheduling informal parlor meetings with members of the clergy. Lynn Schrayer, Vice President Finance, instituted "*B'Yachad*," an innovative program to help raise funds. It requested a $10,000 annual commitment for three years, covering all regular dues, fair share dues, *Kol Nidre* appeal and the annual fundraiser. Several families would commit to this and in its first year, *B'Yachad* raised $33,500 in new contributions. The Men's Club, too, began an innovative program: the first annual Scotch and Bourbon Tasting (but only for members over twenty-one years of age!).

In March, 2005, the Social Action Committee, still under the leadership of Larry and Enid Arnowitz, sponsored a Mitzvah Fair, in which thirty-five social service agencies and charities participated. Congregants were able to learn about different opportunities for community service. An outgrowth of this event was the congregation's annual Mitzvah Day, initially organized by

Rabbi Schwab and Jackie Kotte-Wolle, a day on which members of the congregation would go into the community to perform real deeds of charity. That same month, with Rabbi Schwab's guidance, the synagogue sponsored the first innovative "Ruach Shabbat" program which brought families with young children to the synagogue for Friday night services and dinner.

Rodney Slutzky became Beth El's president in May, 2005. He quickly oversaw several new initiatives and activities. That summer, *Shabbat* services were held in the Blumberg Auditorium while major renovations were undertaken to the Field Family Sanctuary, supervised, once again, by Mae Spitz and with the assistance of Seth Pines. The work consisted of new carpeting, refinishing of the woodwork, and the installation of a fifth chair on either side of the *bimah*. The project was made possible through the generosity of Sisterhood and the Field family. At the same time, serious structural deterioration to the exterior of the sanctuary building was discovered and necessary repairs were carried out over the next year at a cost in excess of $380,000. Thanks to the foresight of previous administrations, adequate reserves existed in the capital improvement fund to cover the cost.

Beth El member Merle Tovian became the Director of Continuing Education during the summer of 2005. The previous February she had been instrumental in forming a women's Rosh Chodesh group. In the Cohen Religious School, however, enrollment was weakening and within the next two years would fall below 320 children. Many felt that some members were enrolling their children in programs at Reform congregations that offered a less intensive schedule of classes. However, Rabbi Kurtz was firm on maintaining a six-hour-per-week program, and the Board of Directors agreed with him. The quality of the school continued to excel and in November Beth El received a Solomon Schechter Award from United Synagogue of Conservative Judaism for Excellence in Education. The decline in school enrollment paralleled a further decline in synagogue membership. Many thought this was due to the high cost of housing on the North Shore or the reduced numbers of young families moving to the suburbs from Chicago. The Membership Committee was particularly concerned by the competition for young families from Reform congregations and by the "aging"[158] of the congregation, a phenomenon which was common across the Conservative movement. Regardless of the causes, membership had fallen to 1,028 families by June, 2005.

In an effort to attract new members, the Membership Committee, under the leadership of Fran Levy and with the assistance of Rabbi Schwab, organized a wine and cheese "*Kabbalat Shabbat* on the Lake," held on August 26, 2005 in the synagogue's beautiful backyard overlooking Lake Michigan. This was a very popular program, attracting more than 300 participants, and would be repeated at least once each summer thereafter. Also, that fall the Board of Directors created the new office of Vice President Membership and the following spring Kim Levy was elected to that office.

Under President Slutzky, several new committees began work in 2005. The Communications Committee, chaired by Lisa Rosenkranz, worked to suggest improved means of communicating with congregants. The committee soon undertook a survey of the congregation and by the fall of 2006 had introduced a "new look" in the synagogue letterhead and logo reflecting Beth El's "new identity." A Governance Committee was also formed to evaluate the manner in which the functioning of the synagogue could be made more efficient and effective. In addition, Larry Arnowitz, then still the chair of the Social Action Committee, reported to the Board on the "very positive effect" Rabbi Schwab was having on social action programs, particularly in connection with the on-going *Vav* class for bar and bat mitzvah students and their parents and in response to the devastation along the Gulf Coast caused by Hurricane Katrina.

Despite the decline in membership, the financial picture in 2006 was bright. The latest financial statements listed the synagogue's total assets at approximately $10 million with long-term debt of less than $1 million. Also, Gertrude Lederman,

158   At this time 35% of the synagogue's membership was above the age of sixty-five; only 6% was between thirty and thirty-nine years of age.

whose family had joined Beth El in 1952, passed away leaving a bequest to the congregation which constituted the largest single gift ever received by the synagogue and which increased the assets of the Endowment Corporation to almost $4 million. [159] In recognition of this magnificent act of generosity, the Board voted to dedicate the synagogue's Continuing Education Program in her memory. However, membership continued to pose a concern, and a special Board meeting held in June, 2006 was devoted entirely to enhancing growth at the synagogue. It was organized with the assistance of the Jewish Federation and led by Julie Webb, a membership consultant with the Union for Reform Judaism.

The Conservative movement was facing its own challenges at this time. In June, 2006, the leader of the movement, Dr. Ismar Schorsch, stepped down after twenty years as Chancellor of the Jewish Theological Seminary. His replacement was Dr. Arnold Eisen, not a rabbi but a world-renowned sociologist at Stanford University, who was looked to for revitalization of the movement. In March, 2007, the new chancellor-elect would make his first public appearance in the Midwest at a special Seminary lecture and forum held at Beth El. In December, 2006, in a matter that caused further controversy within the Conservative movement, the Committee on Jewish Law and Standards of the Rabbinical Assembly, of which Rabbi Kurtz was a member, approved two diametrically opposite opinions of Jewish law: the first reaffirmed traditional *halacha*, which imposed certain restrictions on homosexual behavior and relationships; the second approved normalizing the status of homosexuals within the Conservative movement and its institutions and also condoned same-sex unions. Rabbi Kurtz supported the first opinion and voted against the second. Shortly thereafter, at an open forum at the synagogue to discuss and explain the seemingly contradictory position of the Law Committee, the rabbi clarified the reasons that Beth El, consistent

---

[159] By the end of 2006, Ben Neuhausen announced that the assets of the Endowment Corporation were being invested in the funds professionally managed by the Jewish Federation of Chicago.

with its traditional interpretation of Jewish law, would follow the first of these two opinions.

In the meantime, the 35th World Zionist Congress, the "Parliament of the Jewish People," convened in Jerusalem in the summer of 2006, and Rabbi Kurtz, as president of MERCAZ Olami, was instrumental in negotiating with Israel's Prime Minister Ehud Olmert to form the largest coalition at the Congress. It was a proud moment for the delegates from Beth El as well as their rabbi.

In August, 2006, Ken Levin reported on another unexpected maintenance problem: an underground oil storage tank, a vestige of the old Price mansion, had been located in the backyard near the Gan Sylvia Playground. While no hazards had been identified, the tank and underground contamination were promptly remediated and the playground was renovated. This and other issues facing the House Committee prompted the establishment of a committee to create a Master Plan for the physical development of the synagogue. Levin also announced he would be retiring as executive director. Karen Bieber soon chaired a committee to find a new executive director and Chuck Kahalnik assumed that position in August, 2007.[160] Levin was honored at a special *kiddush* in November of that year. In May, 2007, Rabbi Kurtz had the sad task of informing the congregation of the passing of "my good friend, colleague, congregant and mentor" Rabbi Mordecai Simon. Rabbi Simon was eighty-one years of age at the time of his death and had been a stalwart of Beth El and a friend to the entire Chicago Jewish community for over forty years. Later that year, the Men's Club once again was awarded the prestigious Gold Torch Award from the National Federation of Jewish Men's Club for best overall activities.

Since the middle of 2006, plans were being formulated to recognize the 60th anniversary of Beth El's founding. Len Tenner, Andy Saffir and Richard Rabinowitz were designated co-chairmen for this special occasion. On Yom Kippur in 2007, Rabbi

---

160   A notable first at Beth El occurred on August 18, 2007 when Gabrielle, Janna and Kira Berman became the first set of triplets to celebrate their joint bat mitzvah at the synagogue.

Kurtz,[161] by now the longest-serving spiritual leader in Beth El's history, spoke to the congregation of the significance of the Diamond Jubilee celebrations. Soon thereafter, a "Guide to the Year Long Celebration" was sent to all members. The theme for the celebration was "Celebrating the Journey; *Aloh Na'aleh*" [162] and the logo for the event appeared on all correspondence and bulletins of the synagogue, on festive colorful banners placed in the parking lot and on the synagogue building, and even on special *kippot* made for the occasion. Scheduled throughout the year were many special speakers and a congregational trip to Israel in the spring of 2008 led by Rabbi Kurtz to coincide with the celebration of Israel's 60th anniversary. One of the first events, in December, 2007, was an uplifting, jubilant concert in the Blumberg Auditorium by Neshama Carlebach. Close to 400 people attended in what was called "a moment of pure happiness." The culminating event for the anniversary celebration would be the "Diamond Gala" in the Blumberg Auditorium scheduled for September 7, 2008, a "sparkling" formal dinner dance which would feature the raffle of a diamond necklace and the celebration of Beth El's "multi-faceted" journey.

Sadly, in the midst of these celebrations, the congregation learned of the passing of the last of its original founders. Ruby Blumberg, who with her late husband Harold had been a witness to the entire Beth El story, died on December 31, 2007. Her funeral was held two days later at the synagogue she had helped build. It was truly the end of an era for the synagogue.

Lynn Schrayer became Beth El's twenty-eighth president in 2007. She emphasized her goal of helping members feel more engaged with their synagogue and introduced as an "experiment" at Board meetings the new structure of a "consent agenda," intended to free the meeting from routine administrative matters and allow the directors to address important issues on a more detailed level. One of those issues was the

---

161   Rabbi Kurtz at this time had the honor of being accepted to participate in the intensive study program for rabbis at the Shalom Hartman Institute in Jerusalem.

162   See Numbers 13:30.

future development of the synagogue and soon a special Board meeting was held to deal with the "mission and vision" for the congregation, out of which grew the Education Mission and Vision Task Force chaired by Elise Frost with assistance from Gary Goldman. It would play a critical role in the evolution and development of the synagogue's educational program.

The committee formulating the synagogue's Master Plan was also active. Co-chaired by Richard Becker and Stuart Cohen, the committee expended much thought and effort to develop the initial draft of a Master Plan professionally prepared by Cyrus Subawalla of the Chicago architectural firm of Hammond, Beeby, Rupert, Ainge. It was presented to the congregation at a well-attended open forum in September, 2007. Among its extensive recommendations was the demolition of virtually all the improvements constructed in 1987-88 and their replacement with new structures, including the addition of a second floor to the school building. However, the draft plan was perceived by many as too ambitious and too costly. President Schrayer emphasized that the plan was a "work in progress" and a refined plan was presented to the congregation in March, 2008.

In October, 2007, Fred Sechan, Vice President Ritual, announced that a monthly Carlebach-style *kabbalat Shabbat* service was being introduced, another innovation of Rabbi Schwab. Since his arrival at Beth El, Rabbi Schwab had gained the confidence and affection of the congregation. He had worked closely with young families to promote membership and had developed interesting new programming initiatives. He was held in high esteem by all segments of the congregation. In December, 2007, he led a "sold out" family trip to Israel. In another break with Beth El precedent, in the spring of 2008 the Board approved an extension of Rabbi Schwab's contract for five years, through the summer of 2014. In connection with this extension, the congregation acquired the house at 1168 Wade Street for use by the Schwab family. In addition, his title was changed first to Associate Rabbi and then in 2009 to merely "Rabbi" in recognition of his increasing responsibilities and experience.

As the celebration of the 60th anniversary of the synagogue progressed, changes in key personnel would remind the congregation of the continuously evolving story of Beth El. In the spring of 2008, Cheryl Banks, after twenty years as the director of the Gray Cultural and Learning Center, announced her retirement. Aaron Klein, who for the previous decade had maintained at the Cohen Religious School the high academic standards which had become a Beth El tradition, also announced he would retire at the end of the school year.[163] A search committee chaired by Joyce Fox soon recommended inviting Karen Raizen of the McHenry County Jewish Congregation in Crystal Lake, Illinois, to serve as the new director of the Religious School beginning in July 2008. As had been done repeatedly over the past sixty years, the congregation was preparing for the future.[164]

---

[163]   Klein, who years earlier had been a contestant on the popular television game show "Jeopardy," would continue to teach in the Beth El schools.

[164]   The growth of the Jewish community in the northern suburbs of Chicago was also evidenced by the opening in 2008 of Mizrahi Grill, a kosher Israeli restaurant in the Crossroads Shopping Center in Highland Park.

NORTH SUBURBAN SYNAGOGUE BETH EL

1175 Sheridan Road
Highland Park, Illinois

CONTINUING EDUCATION PROGRAM

1971 - 1972 *BULLETIN*

Samuel H. Dresner, Rabbi
Philip L. Lipis, Rabbi Emeritus
Reuven Frankel, Cantor
Rabbi David B. Saltzman, Educational Director
Mr. Theodore C. Bloch, Educational Vice President
Dr. Michael Radnor, Chairman

Continuing Education Program brochure for 1971-1972. Adult education was an important aspect of Rabbi Samuel H. Dresner's vision for Beth El. The instructors for this year included Professor Moses Shulvas, Rabbi Byron Sherwin, Dr. Elizer Berkovitz, Cantor Reuven Frankel and Rabbi Dresner. The brochure also announced a "Heschel Weekend" in October, 1971, featuring Rabbi Abraham Joshua Heschel and Dr. Hans Morgenthau. (Beth El Archives)

THE JEWISH THEOLOGICAL SEMINARY OF AMERICA
3080 BROADWAY · NEW YORK, NEW YORK 10027
212 RIVERSIDE 8-8000

OFFICE OF THE CHANCELLOR

CABLE ADDRESS: SEMINARY, NEW YORK

March 1, 1973

Dear Mr. and Mrs. Rosenblum:

I am in receipt of the very kind invitation to join
you on March 25th for the dedication of the Maxwell Abbell
Library at North Suburban Synagogue Beth El. If it were
at all possible, I would plan to be with you at that time
but, unfortunately, in this first year of my administration
of the Seminary, I find my time overcommitted for most
days, March 25th among them.

My inability to be present does not reflect in any
way either on the warmth of my good wishes on this important
occasion, or on my great respect for the Abbell Family, and
for the memory of Maxwell Abbell and his abiding contributions
to the survival of Jewish learning in America. In future
years, as historians chronicle the means by which the
foundations of a strong American Jewry were forged with
links to the heritage from our ancestors, they will be
able to point to Maxwell Abbell's support as vital to the
enterprise. The Maxwell Abbell Library which you are
dedicating will stand as a visible symbol of this great
undertaking.

I send all of you, and particularly Mrs. Maxwell Abbell,
my greetings and best wishes on this event which is so
significant for you, and for all of us here at the Seminary.

Sincerely,

Gerson D. Cohen

Mr. and Mrs. Paul R. Rosenblum
2401 St. Johns Avenue
Highland Park, Illinois

Letter of Dr. Gerson D. Cohen, Chancellor of the Jewish Theological Seminary, to Miriam and Paul Rosenblum on the occasion of the dedication of the Maxwell Abbell Library at Beth El on March 25, 1973. The Library has grown into one of the largest of any Conservative congregation and is an essential component of the Joseph and Mae Gray Cultural and Learning Center. (Beth El Archives)

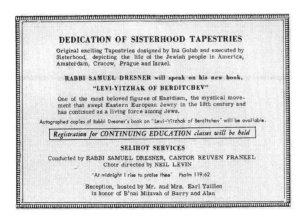

DEDICATION OF SISTERHOOD TAPESTRIES

Original exciting Tapestries designed by Ina Golub and executed by Sisterhood, depicting the life of the Jewish people in America, Amsterdam, Cracow, Prague and Israel.

RABBI SAMUEL DRESNER will speak on his new book,

"LEVI-YITZHAK OF BERDITCHEV"

One of the most beloved figures of Hasidism, the mystical movement that swept Eastern European Jewry in the 18th century and has continued as a living force among Jews.

Autographed copies of Rabbi Dresner's book on "Levi-Yitzhak of Berditchev" will be available.

Registration for CONTINUING EDUCATION classes will be held

SELIHOT SERVICES

Conducted by RABBI SAMUEL DRESNER, CANTOR REUVEN FRANKEL
Choir directed by NEIL LEVIN

"At midnight I rise to praise thee" Psalm 119:62

Reception, hosted by Mr. and Mrs. Earl Yaillen
in honor of B'nai Mitzvah of Barry and Alan

Notice of the dedication ceremony on September 7, 1974 for the tapestries created by members of the Sisterhood. These works of art were displayed in the foyer of the Sanctuary until 2016. (Beth El Archives)

NORTH SUBURBAN SYNAGOGUE
BETH EL SISTERHOOD

presents

"The Marriage Go-Round"

A delightful evening of entertainment

- **Saturday Evening**   **December 6, 1975**
- **Sunday Evening**   **December 7, 1975**

```
Samuel H. Dresner, Rabbi
Philip L. Lipis, Rabbi Emeritus
Reuven Frankel, Cantor
```

Program for "The Marriage Go-Round" presented by the Beth El Sisterhood on December 6 and 7, 1975. An active affiliate of the congregation, the Sisterhood not only made significant contributions to the synagogue, but it also provided numerous programs for congregants' entertainment. The cast for this program included many longtime congregants, including Zella Ludwig, Sally Stiefel, Marilyn Ruekberg, Pearl White, Mort Taxy, Dan Tauman, Michael Cahr and Howard Lidov. (Beth El Archives)

NORTH SUBURBAN SYNAGOGUE BETH EL

MEN'S CLUB PRESENTS

Cantor David Kusevitsky

Acclaimed one of the foremost interpreters of Hebrew liturgical music, Cantor Kusevitsky is an unforgettable experience.

JEWISH MUSIC FESTIVAL 78

produced by the

BETH EL MUSIC COMMITTEE

Honoring Israel's 30th Anniversary

Wednesday, May 10, 1978, 8:00 o'clock, p.m.

Beth El Sanctuary

featuring

Cantor Reuven Frankel

with the Beth El Choral Ensemble

also featuring

The North Shore Chamber Choir

conducted by Carol Hyman

1175 Sheridan Road, Highland Park, Ill./Public Welcome

Program for the Men's Club Music Festival on May 10, 1978, featuring Cantor David Kusevitsky and Beth El's Cantor Reuven Frankel. The annual music festival has been a Beth El tradition for many years. Elliot Mirman was the chairman of this festival and Lawrence Block chaired the synagogue's Music Committee. (Beth El Archives)

NORTH SUBURBAN SYNAGOGUE BETH EL
and
STATE OF ISRAEL BONDS
proudly honor

Rabbi and Mrs. Mordecai Simon

Consistently a strong supporter of State of Israel Bonds, the synagogue honored Rabbi Mordecai and Maxine Simon at a tribute dinner in 1978 which featured Admiral Elmo Zumwalt, Jr., former Chief of Naval Operations for the U.S. Navy, as guest speaker. (Beth El Archives)

The planning committee for an Israel Bonds tribute dinner honoring Cantor Reuven and Penina Frankel c.1970s. Standing (L-R): Sig Feiger, Mimi Feiger, Bernard Alpert, Albert Kopin, Abby Block and Myrna Kopin. Seated (L-R): Penina Frankel, Cantor Reuven Frankel and Lawrence Block. (Beth El Archives)

143

Culminating the Torah writing project on June 15, 1980 was the dedication of the new scroll. Arthur Rubinoff, who chaired the project, holds the new Sefer Torah while synagogue founders Benjamin and Gertrude Harris recite appropriate prayers as Rabbi William H. Lebeau looks on. (Beth El Archives)

Robert and Yadelle Sklare receive an award c.1979 believed to be from Israel Bonds. This photo was taken outside of the Sager Beit HaMidrash in what is now the Lidov Family Memorial Alcove. In the background is the *Etz Chaim* dedication which was removed several years later. Standing (L-R): unidentified; Arnold Kaplan, synagogue president; Sam Rade, Executive Director; Robert Sklare; unidentified; Jean Bernstein, Sisterhood president; unidentified; Rabbi William H. Lebeau and Sig Feiger. Seated is Yadelle Sklare. (Beth El Archives)

The program for "Katz," an original musical production written by Roberta Caplan and Sandy Fishman, held on June 16 and 17, 1984. A take-off on "Cats," the cast and orchestra were composed entirely of congregants. This was one of a series of musical fundraising events held at the synagogue during the 1980s and 1990s. (Beth El Archives)

Herb Isaacs, Shelly Braver and Ed Shapiro perform in "Katz." (Courtesy of Ellen Lavin; Beth El Archives)

The groundbreaking ceremony on September 14, 1986 for the Posen Rabbinic and Administrative Wing in memory of Sam and Michael Posen. The new addition to the synagogue's facilities housed the offices of the clergy and the administrative staff, allowing the ground floor of the Price mansion to be the location of the Gray Cultural and Learning Center. (L-R): Gerald Buckman, Rabbi William H. Lebeau, Faye Posen and Ken Levin, synagogue president. (Beth El Archives)

The completed Posen Rabbinic and Administrative Wing c.1988. (Photo by Sharon Grossman; Beth El Archives)

CONTRIBUTING WRITERS
Sally Stiefel
Fred Caplan
Rosalind Nachman
Carol Linch

"SATURDAY MORNING" TAP DANCE
Lorraine Chase

MAKE UP
Phyllis Cohodes

TICKETS
Art Cohen
Izzy Mann

PUBLICITY
David Brimm

PRINTING
Mort Taxy

VIDEO
Ted Banks

GLOVES
Stiebel Caterers

COSTUMES
Myrna Schwartz
Ruth Braver

SET DESIGN & BUILDER
Ed Schwartz   Frank Young Co., Inc. · Back Drop Foil
Myrna Schwartz   J.B.S. Builders · Cubes

ARRANGEMENTS
Caryn Garber
Phyllis Fischel

North Suburban Synagogue Beth El
1948-1988

40th *Happy Birthday*

Presenting

1988
LET'S CELEBRATE!
SUNDAY, JUNE 12, 1988
7:00 P.M.

WRITTEN & DIRECTED BY
Roberta Caplan
Edward Shapiro

STAGED & CHOREOGRAPHED BY
Roberta Caplan

PRODUCERS
Ed Schwartz
Myrna Schwartz

Program for the 40th Anniversary Celebration, "1988 - Let's Celebrate," presented on June 12, 1988. Written by Roberta Caplan and Ed Shapiro, it was another of the grand musicals produced as a fundraising event during the 1980s and 1990s. (Beth El Archives)

Rabbi Vernon Kurtz makes a surprise appearance at the 40th Anniversary Celebration on June 12, 1988, shortly before he officially became the rabbi of Beth El. (Courtesy of Ellen Lavin; Beth El Archives)

OFFICERS

Howard M. Turner, President
Leonard R. Tenner, Vice-President - Administration
Sandra M. Brown, Vice-President - Education
Jeffrey Wohlstadter, Vice-President - Finance
Lawrence R. Weiner, Vice-President - Ritual
Michael H. Nadler, Treasurer
Mae L. Spitz, Financial Secretary
Richard K. Janger, Secretary

INSTALLATION COMMITTEE

Harold R. Blumberg   Albert Kopin, Chairman
David Brimm   Kenneth S. Levin
Dr. Gerald Buckman   Howard I. Lidov
Eli Field   Zella Ludwig
Caryn Garber   Irving Robbin
Harold Gorin

1948 - 1988

North Suburban Synagogue Beth El

Program

Installation of
Rabbi Vernon Kurtz

Sunday
December 11, 1988
Tevet 4, 5749
7:30 p.m.

Program for the installation ceremony of Rabbi Vernon Kurtz on December 11, 1988. Formally installed by Rabbi Kass Abelson of Minneapolis, Rabbi Kurtz served as Beth El's fifth and longest-serving senior rabbi. (Beth El Archives)

148

Harold Blumberg stands in the Field Family Sanctuary in 1998 in front of the *aron kodesh* with its doors designed by world-renowned designer Ludwig Wolpert. One of the most active of the original founders, Blumberg was key to the growth of the congregation throughout the 1950s and 1960s. (Photo by Vicki Grayland; Beth El Archives)

Rabbi Vernon Kurtz and Lynn Schrayer participate in the community-wide 2004 Walk with Israel at McCormick Place on Chicago's lakefront. Support of Israel was a key aspect of Rabbi Kurtz's rabbinate. (Beth El Archives)

The Sager Beit Midrash following its renovation in 2017. (Beth El Archives)

Beth El's Senior Rabbis

Maurice I. Kliers
1948 - 1950

Philip L. Lipis
1951 - 1969

Samuel H. Dresner
1969 - 1977

William H. Lebeau
1978 - 1987

Beth El's Senior Rabbis

Vernon H. Kurtz
1988-2019

Michael Schwab
2019 -

Beth El's Cantors
(continued on next page)

Cantor Stanley Martin
1948-1953

Beth El's Cantors

Cantor Jordan Cohen
1953-1969

Cantor Reuven Frankel
1970-1979

Cantor Eliahu Treistman
1979-1980

Cantor Aryeh Finklestein
1981-1984

Beth El's Cantors

Cantor Larry Josefovitz
1985-1987

Hazzan Henry Rosenblum
1987-1998

Hazzan Larry B. Goller
1998-2015

Hazzan Benjamin A. Tisser
2015-

VII. RECESSION AND RECOVERY
(2008–2018)

Beth El's 60th Anniversary "Diamond Gala" celebration on September 7, 2008 was a social as well as a financial success. Over 325 congregants were in attendance and more than $67,000 was raised for Beth El's programs. But by this time it was apparent that the economic picture, not only in Highland Park but across the country, was becoming very bleak. This was the beginning of what some would call the Great Recession, and it would impact Beth El, the Highland Park community and the entire country in many ways over the next several years. Some congregants would lose their jobs and some would face the foreclosure of their home mortgages. Within a few months, the synagogue's Membership Committee, chaired by JoAnne Blumberg Axelrod, instituted the Beth El Community Network, a service intended to assist congregants in locating job opportunities. That was followed by the formation of a support group for spouses of those out of work, or as would be publicized, for those who "are on a career path." The Men's Club held a special program on "Surviving the Economic Downturn" and Sisterhood made a special gift of $25,000 to help balance the synagogue's budget.

In the spring of 2009, Treasurer Leonard Weitz reported that the "current financial crisis affects every Beth El family" and for the first time in many years annual dues were not increased, even though dues revenue had dropped by more than 8% and requests for financial assistance had increased. (Dues had reached $2,545 per year by this time.) Ron Goldberg, Financial Vice President, reported that the *Kol Nidre* appeal in October of 2008 was more than 15% below the amount raised the previous year, and overall fundraising was at least 20% below the prior year's numbers. And the "Big Event," which was held in May, 2009, "Beth El's Got Talent," raised only $4,000.

The sharp economic downturn also affected the synagogue's

schools. Enrollment in all the schools was down, with less than 300 children attending classes in the Cohen Religious School and less than 120 students in the Sokol Hebrew High School. Within two years enrollment would decline even further, with only 196 and 99 students enrolled respectively in these programs. By the following spring, declining registration in the Steinberg Pre-School resulted in the elimination of afternoon sessions; enrollment, which a few years earlier had reached almost 200, dropped to only seventy-six children in the fall of 2009. And although the Master Plan Committee had hoped to implement a major fundraising program in the fall of 2008, it was apparent that funds would not be forthcoming. Officially, the Master Plan of 2007 was "on hold"; in reality, it was abandoned.

The economy and education: these would be the major challenges facing the congregation for the next several years. But despite difficulties encountered, Beth El would endure the impact of the economic crisis and continue to flourish in its multitude of educational, ritual and cultural programs. Initially, many of the activities at the synagogue seemed hardly affected by the dour economic situation. Andrew Brown chaired a new Human Resources Task Force which by December, 2008 had produced an extensive Employee Handbook detailing work hours, vacation and overtime policies, lunch periods, standards of personal appearance and hygiene, and many other subjects. In June of 2008, in an effort to grow the synagogue's membership, Beth El for the first time sponsored a booth at the Greater Chicago Jewish Folk Festival. That fall Kim Levy, Vice President Membership, reported fifty-five new families had joined the congregation, although there also had been a noticeable drop in existing memberships. And as part of the Youth Commission report in August, Nancy Becker happily announced the *auf-ruf* and forthcoming marriage of Ali Schlamowitz, Youth Director, to Mr. Michael Drumm. The new couple would rent the synagogue's townhouse on Judson Avenue after Rabbi Schwab's family moved into the newly acquired residence on Wade Street.

The fall of 2008 brought Rachel Kamin to Beth El from Temple Israel in West Bloomfield, Michigan as the new director of the Gray Cultural and Learning Center. She quickly set out to upgrade the technology in the Susan Fisher Glick Research Center and to spearhead other innovations in the operations for that important facility of the synagogue. Within a few years, she would greatly expand the programing of the Cultural and Learning Center and also assume responsibility for the displays in the Rissman Family Kol Ami Museum. Also that year, the Men's Club organized "Shabbat At Lieberman's," the Jewish senior life facility in Skokie, whereby members and their families on a monthly basis assisted residents in various aspects of *Shabbat* services and rituals, a program which continues to the present. Men's Club also began participating in the Highland Park Park District's summer softball league. In the fall of 2008, Rabbi Kurtz was awarded the inaugural Rabbi Mordecai Simon Award by the Chicago Board of Rabbis. The award, named in memory of the longtime and highly respected Executive Vice President of that organization and former member of the Beth El family, recognized outstanding services to the community by its recipient, truly a deserving honor for Rabbi Kurtz.

In January, 2009, the Education Mission and Vision Task Force, with input from over thirty-five synagogue members and educators, produced a written report of the broad mission for Jewish education that should be implemented at Beth El, including classical Jewish study, Hebrew language, Jewish life and culture, Israel and social action. The report was distributed to all members of the Board of Directors and all committees of the Board of Education; it would have a significant impact on Beth El's educational programing in the coming years.

During the spring of 2009, the Ritual Committee prepared laminated cards to be placed in the pews of the Field Family Sanctuary containing the "NSSBE Guide to Shabbat Services."[165] In May, the committee oversaw the installation of a new and colorful *parochet* for the ark in the Field Family Sanc-

---

[165] Three years later, Richard Schlosberg, Vice President Ritual, would oversee the preparation of a similar guide to weekday services for the Sager Bet HaMidrash.

tuary; handmade in Israel, it was a gift of the Shalowitz and Cowans families in memory of Sydney Shalowitz. Soon thereafter, a white *parochet* for use on the High Holidays was installed, a gift of Yadelle Sklare in memory of her husband, Robert Sklare. Also that spring, Tammie Roth, who had served as Director of the Steinberg Pre-School since 1992 and had elevated the Pre-School's program to new heights, left her position at Beth El. Ellen Nathan, chair of the Pre-School Committee, worked diligently with Interim Director Libby Goldenberg to see that the Pre-School completed the school year smoothly.

Steve Abrams was chosen to serve as Beth El's president in May, 2009. He soon instituted the electronic distribution of monthly officers' reports, notices of meetings and minutes to Board members, both to save postage and paper and to permit directors' meetings to constitute a forum for strategic planning and discussion. One of the first changes made by the Board was motivated by the report of the Education Mission and Vision Task Force: the creation of the position of Director of Youth & Family Programming. Ali Drumm was soon chosen to fill this position. Within the next few months she was able to institute a great deal of coordination in programing among the Youth Community, the Gray Cultural and Learning Center, and the Lederman Continuing Education Program. Also as a result of that report, the oversight of the synagogue's schools was allocated between Rabbis Kurtz and Schwab.

The summer of 2009 was quite eventful. At the annual Jewish Theological Seminary dinner in Chicago on June 18, 2009, attended by many congregants, Hazzan Goller was honored with the prestigious Hazzan Putterman Cantorial Leadership Award from the Seminary. The following month he participated in the historic mission of 100 members of the Cantors Assembly to Poland for concerts and touring. Also that summer, pursuant to the recommendation of the Pre-School Director Search Committee, chaired by Elise Frost, Caron Knopoff became the new director of the Steinberg Pre-School. At her introduction to the Board in September, she summarized her goals for the Pre-School: to create for the students pleasant Jewish memories and to instill in them pride in being Jewish. She would serve in that position with great effectiveness for the next seven years, working diligently to improve the curriculum and other aspects of the school. In the Sokol Hebrew High School, Randi Newman undertook a revamping of administrative as well as educational elements of the program. As an important improvement to the physical facilities of the High School, the Levin Seminar Room, filled with the most current educational technology, was dedicated that fall in memory of longtime member Dr. Jacob Levin and in honor of his wife Betty Levin.

Heavy rains deluged the Chicago area during the summer of 2009, which was the primary cause of the collapse of the bluff overlooking Lake Michigan at the northeast corner of the synagogue's property, precisely where Gan Sylvia, the Pre-School playground, was located. For the next two years, the repair of the bluff, the removal of fallen trees and invasive species, the installation of proper drainage and the rebuilding of the playground were a constant focus of the Board of Directors. The total cost for this unexpected project exceeded $200,000; Lisa Rosenkranz, Vice President Administration, with major assistance from Chuck Kahalnik, oversaw all the work. Kahalnik also assisted Seth Pines and Mae Spitz that year in overseeing the carpeting and painting of the school building's hallways and he would do the same for the carpeting of the Paset Lounge the following year. Kahalnik also had Wi-Fi installed in the school building, taught classes, was responsible for the kitchen and even prepared meals for numerous synagogue functions, all in addition to his duties as Executive Director in the synagogue's office. At the Board meeting in October, 2009, he was roundly complimented for his outstanding work and his "can do" attitude.

For the High Holidays in 2009, over 500 children were registered for different reorganized and revamped children services, including a parent/children family service at the synagogue, led by Gail and Joel Tenner, that attracted over 200 participants. In November, a State of Israel Bond reception honored Sisterhood, recognizing the important role that affiliate plays in the life of the congregation. One enduring program of Sisterhood was, and still is, the Torah Fund classes taught by Beth El's clergy and professional staff and organized for many years by Marilyn Lewis.[166] Another innovative and popular program was a series of cooking classes led by Laura Frankel, then the Executive Chef for Spertus Kosher Catering. And soon Mahjongg, under the direction of Michelle Krawitz, would be offered as a source of entertainment to Sisterhood members.

Despite the uncertain economy during this period, the cultural aspects of the synagogue were not neglected. Many distinguished authors and scholars participated in continuing education programs or endowed speakers' forums or other special events at the synagogue. Included among these notable individuals were Ruth Messinger of the American Jewish World Service, Dr. Tovah Hartman, an Israeli scholar and founder of *Kehillat Shira Hadasha*, a modern Orthodox congregation in Jerusalem, Dr. David Golinkin of the Schetcher Institute in Jerusalem, and Dr. Jonathan Sarna of Brandeis University.

Still, membership in the congregation continued to decline, reaching 1,035 families in the fall of 2009. The following spring, the Board of Directors was surprised to learn that the congregation had only two member families below the age of thirty and only thirty-seven member families between the ages of thirty and forty, a symptom of the aging of the congregation and of the Conservative movement in general. Determined to address this problem, President Abrams proposed a new dues structure to encourage young families to join the synagogue, including the elimination of the "infamous" Building Fund, which had been a mainstay of the dues structure since its introduction in 1960. His proposal was soon adopted.

In 2009, Fran Sherman became the first woman to serve as Vice President Ritual and she oversaw a full agenda of items which benefitted the congregation. Under her leadership the Ritual Committee updated the Standards and Practices booklet for religious rituals at Beth El, which was distributed to con-

---

[166] In 2013, Lewis received the Valued Volunteer Award from the Central Great Lakes Region of Women's League for Conservative Judaism.

gregants in the summer of 2010. The Committee also investigated and eventually acquired transliterated *siddurim* for use by worshippers not knowledgeable in Hebrew. With the assistance of Michael Shartiag, the Ritual Committee implemented computer software to track weekly Torah reading assignments to assure smooth Torah services on *Shabbat* mornings. Also in 2010, the Ritual Committee recommended extending the contract of Hazzan Goller for another five years.

In the spring of 2010, Karen Bieber, chair of the By-Laws Committee, proposed, and the Board approved, a series of amendments to the synagogue by-laws, including extending the term of office for officers to two years, thereby formalizing what had been the practice at the synagogue for close to fifty years. That summer, as a result of the efforts of Rabbi Kurtz, who by that time also served as Adjunct Professor of Rabbinic Studies at the Spertus Institute of Jewish Studies, the synagogue formalized a relationship with the Spertus Institute making Beth El its "home on the North Shore."[167] This was another achievement of the Education Mission and Vision: to make education a life-long experience.

By the fall of 2010, the economic crisis, although not resolved, began to ease, and with it came the congregation's increased participation in fundraising and increased enrollment in its schools. JoAnne Blumberg Axelrod announced that eighty-five new families had joined Beth El, due in large part to the elimination of the Building Fund. Also, the Steinberg Pre-School, which ended its 2009-2010 school year with a Bubbie and Zaide Shabbat attended by over 100 grandparents, saw enrollment for the 2010-2011 school year grow by more than 20%.

At the High Holidays that fall, with the strong encouragement of Rabbi Kurtz, *Machzor Lev Shalem*, newly published by the Rabbinical Assembly, replaced the Silverman High Holiday Prayer Book that had been in use since the earliest days of the synagogue. In the *Kol Beth-El* bulletin of August, 2010, Rabbi

---

167   Shortly thereafter the formal name of the Spertus Institute was changed to the Spertus Institute for Jewish Learning and Leadership.

Kurtz provided an introduction to the new volume, saying he was confident "the Machzor will enhance our prayer services, the spirituality of our Holy Days and make the experience a meaningful one for all." The new *machzor* for the most part maintained the traditional prayers for Rosh Hashanah and Yom Kippur, but what was most appealing to the congregation was the inclusion of modern English readings and a friendlier English translation of the Hebrew prayers.[168] Following the High Holidays, Rabbi Kurtz was granted a well-deserved four-month sabbatical, most of which the Kurtzes spent in Jerusalem, where they had recently acquired their own apartment. Before he left, however, the rabbi received another prestigious award: the Julius Rosenwald Memorial Award from the Jewish Federation of Metropolitan Chicago, its highest award for community service. It was a most meaningful honor for Rabbi Kurtz.

At the Board of Directors meeting on December 2, 2010, the directors unanimously approved one of the most significant changes to the educational structure at Beth El. The new plan was a direct outgrowth of the Education Mission and Vision Report issued almost two years earlier and had been developed by Rabbis Kurtz and Schwab with input from the Board of Education and the vice presidents of education. The plan called for the elimination of the positions of director of the Cohen Religious School and director of the Sokol Hebrew High School, to be replaced by one Director of Formal Education who would also oversee the programming of the Steinberg Pre-School. Simultaneously, the position of Director of Youth & Family Programming would be replaced with a Director of Informal Education, responsible for the Gray Cultural and Learning Center, the Gertrude Lederman Continuing Education Program and the Youth program. In a letter to the congregation, the rabbis and President Abrams explained that the new educational structure would enable the congregation "to hire two

---

[168] With the introduction of the new *machzor*, the Ritual Committee was faced with the question of what to do with the thousands of old Silverman books that were now out of date. Fran Sherman soon announced a partial solution: 300 of them had been shipped to the developing Jewish community in Uganda.

Directors, each a master educator,.... to create and implement our synagogue's educational strategy." The objectives of the plan would include the development of a strong, integrated curriculum from pre-school through high school and better coordination and integration of all the educational programs at the synagogue. The plan was a renewal of the congregation's historic commitment to educational programing at the highest level.[169]

In April, 2011, Ali Drumm was invited to become the Director of Informal Education.[170] Soon Matt Levitt was hired to serve as Associate Youth Director. That summer, Karen Raizen left Beth El, soon to become the educational director of Congregation Bonai Shalom in Boulder, Colorado, and Randi Newman, who had become administrator of the Sokol Hebrew High School nineteen years earlier, announced her retirement. Larry Pachter, chairman of the search committee for a new director of the schools, recommended, and the Board approved, bringing Alicia Gejman, educational director at West Suburban Temple Har Zion in River Forest, to Beth El as the Director of Formal Education. A native of Argentina, Gejman had made *aliyah* at age eighteen and earned her bachelor's degree from Bar-Ilan University and a master's degree from Hebrew University. She moved to the United States in 1987 and would eventually earn the degree of Doctor of Science in Jewish Studies from the Spertus Institute in Chicago.

Andrew Brown became Beth El's thirtieth president in May, 2011. The new president quickly announced a series of task forces to deal with a variety of issues: bar/bat mitzvah program review, programming for seniors, increasing the number of Torah readers, and technology. He also directed the House

---

[169]   Apparently not everyone in the congregation was enamored with this plan, and at the next Board meeting, President Abrams decried the increased lack of civility in emails and oral comments the Board was receiving and he called upon community leaders to cease "personal attacks, name calling and inappropriate accusation and language" in discussing Beth El issues.

[170]   Holder of a master's degree from the Spertus Institute, in 2013 Drumm was awarded the prestigious title of Conservative Jewish Educator ("CJE") by the Jewish Educators Assembly.

Committee to work with Chuck Kahalnik to develop a capital maintenance and replacement plan for the physical plant of the synagogue: a "road map" for proper annual budgeting for anticipated capital needs. He also announced that beginning in the fall of 2011 background checks would be performed on all current and future synagogue employees, noting that this was a "prudent security measure in these times." By the end of the year, he was able to report no negative information had been discovered in any of those checks.[171]

Soon, Nancy Krent, Vice President Administration, was able to announce the renovation and improvement of the Natkin Seminar Room and the Grossinger-Brickman Activity Center, both having been well used for more than twenty years. She also oversaw the remodeling of the Judson Avenue townhouse, which was rented out so that the "rents will help the budget." In addition, a new audio system was installed in the Field Family Sanctuary, a gift of Ernest Smolen in memory of his son, Hazzan Alan Smolen. And an updated and improved Internet website, designed by Kathy Stinson and Pam Schlosberg, with capability for online payments and donations, was activated.

By the fall of 2011, the new educational structure was showing results. Alicia Gejman had consolidated the school's offices, reviewed and began the revision of school policies, started the "overhaul" of the Hebrew curricula, and sought to hire only the best teachers. She also met frequently with Ali Drumm and Rachel Kamin to coordinate the formal and informal educational activities of the congregation. By this time, the *Vav* class, the weekly session for children preparing to celebrate their bar or bat mitzvah, along with their parents, had been renamed the *"Gesher"* ("bridge") class to reflect the adjustment made in the numbering system for Hebrew classes in the Cohen Religious School.

At this time, some individuals in the congregation expressed a desire to find a more intimate and creative outlet for individ-

---

171   The October, 2011 Board meeting began, as all of them did, with a *d'var Torah* which was particularly moving and memorable as Ruth Fischer recounted her personal experiences in Germany on Kristallnacht, November 9, 1938.

ual talents. In discussions in 2011 with Merle Tovian, Director of Adult Education, and Rachel Kamin of the Gray Cultural and Learning Center, a program entitled "Writers Beit Midrash" was started, involving a small group of congregants who met every other week to share and critique their own personal writings. It was not unusual for some of their works to be published in *East on Central*, the Highland Park literary magazine, and other publications. Another outgrowth of those discussions was the "Artists Beit Midrash," a summer program commenced in 2014. After studying Jewish texts with master educator Jane Shapiro,[172] the participants would create works of art based on what they had learned, many of which would then be displayed in the Rissman Kol Ami Collection, curated by master artist Judith Joseph. The first of these exhibits, in November 2014, was entitled "Artist as *Kohen*: Transmitting Holiness." This endeavor created a new dimension for adult educational programming at the synagogue.[173] Both programs were administered by Marcie Eskin, Librarian and Informal Education Coordinator.

In the fall of 2011, Beth El's USY group completed a project that had begun seven years earlier: the collection of 1.5 million pennies to honor the memory of the 1.5 million Jewish children murdered in the Holocaust. The proceeds of that collection drive, $15,000, were donated to the Illinois Holocaust Museum and Education Center in Skokie in an appropriate ceremony in January, 2012. Meanwhile, the programs for the youth of the synagogue were growing. Audra Kaplan, chair of the Youth Committee, reported in the fall of 2012 that over 350 children were participating in the five youth programs of the synagogue: the M&M Club, the Shalom Club, Kadima, USY and the newest program, PB&J (Peer Buddies and Judaism), a program designed for senior students to work with children with special needs.

---

172   In 2017, Jane Shapiro would be a recipient of the prestigious Covenant Award from the Covenant Foundation, a program established by the Crown Family Philanthropies to honor outstanding Jewish educators and to support creative approaches to programming in Jewish education.

173   The exhibitors in that initial exhibition were Lois Barr, Sam Bernstein, Sylvia Dresser, Nessia Frank, Judith Joseph, Ruti Modlin, Lilach Schrag, Judy Solomon, Linda Carol Sonin, Leah Sosewitz and Sandy Starkman.

And Richard Schlosberg, Vice President Ritual, announced that the Ritual Committee had approved the concept of holding a seder at the synagogue on the second night of Passover, but postponed that activity until the spring of 2013.[174]

The general economic downturn dragged on through 2011. Membership in the congregation continued to drop and stood at 1,019 by the end of the year. Fundraising goals again were not being met. In an attempt to deal with this adverse situation, Lisa Rosenkranz, now Vice President Finance, and others in the congregation had met for some time with the Alford Group, a professional fundraising organization, to investigate the possibility of undertaking a major fundraising campaign to bolster the synagogue's finances. By the beginning of 2012, Rosenkranz reported it was clear that any such campaign "would meet with limited success." Rather, she was working to hire a part-time development person to assist in the "regular" fundraising activities that needed to be maintained by the synagogue. Within a short time, Nancy Kekst was hired to fill that position. The synagogue also hired Avram Pachter as a part-time catering manager to assist Chuck Kahalnik with kitchen duties, a position that became full-time by 2012.[175] Within a year, Beth El's "Circle of Life" catering service was producing excellent results, both culinary and financial. As 2011 drew to a close, Rabbi Kurtz was again honored as the recipient of the Rabbi Mordecai Waxman Memorial Rabbinic & Community Leadership Award at the World Council of Conservative/Masorti Synagogue's "An Evening of Tribute" held at the Jewish Theological Seminary in New York.[176]

At the beginning of 2012, after months of planning, electronic signage consisting of 42" flat screens were installed at each primary entrance to the synagogue to assist visitors in

---

174   Although publicized for Passover in the spring of 2013, the second seder at the synagogue was cancelled for lack of adequate participation.

175   Pachter would leave Beth El in 2014 to become Food Service Director at the Bernard Zell Anshe Emet Day School in Chicago but would return to Beth El at the behest of the synagogue in the fall of 2015 as Director of Hospitality.

176   By the end of 2012, Rabbi Kurtz took on a further national responsibility when he became president of the American Zionist Movement.

finding their way about the buildings and to inform congregants of upcoming programs. Karen Bieber became chair of the Ba'al Korei Institute, serving with Greg Pestine, who assumed the duties of coordinator of Torah readings. Bieber would soon reinvigorate that program and announce that over 150 individuals had served as a Torah reader at least twice during the prior year. Also, Ali Drumm oversaw several impactful programs in January of that year, including "Remembering Wannsee," presented by Joyce Witt to commemorate the 70th anniversary of the formalization of the Nazi's "Final Solution" for European Jewry, and "Tu B'Shvat Rocks," a family concert featuring Shira Klein and her Shir-La-La Band. Later that year, Drumm began administering the HUGS program, a joint effort developed by Rabbi Schwab and Cantor Steve Stoehr of Congregation Beth Shalom in Northbrook for families with children with special needs. Over the next five years, this program would grow to include Moriah Congregation in Deerfield, North Shore Congregation Israel in Glencoe, and nine other Conservative and Reform congregations on the North Shore.

Recognizing the economic turmoil but remaining true to his conviction that "program drives the budget; the budget does not drive the program," President Brown proposed a budget for 2012-2013 "to fit our current size": it contemplated expenditures of $3.6 million, down approximately $500,000 from prior years. He was able to report that Beth El, despite the economic environment, was in a sound financial situation with an available line of credit at Northern Trust Company should a need for cash arise. Also in 2012, Matt Levitt announced his departure from the Beth El Youth Community to work full-time at Ramah in the Rockies. Soon Samantha Isenstein became the new Youth Community Director.

In the spring of 2012, the Rabbinical Assembly published *The Observant Life*, a compilation of *halacha* for Conservative Judaism. Rabbi Kurtz was the author of the chapter on Civic Morality. In May, Beth El, with its unique combination of architectures, was featured in "Synagogues By Bus: North Shore Modern," a program of the Chicago Architectural Foundation, a distinct honor for the congregation. And during the summer, the roof and ceiling of the rear portico overlooking the synagogue's backyard, part of the original Price mansion constructed 100 years earlier, were rebuilt.

By this time plans were well underway to commemorate the synagogue's 65th anniversary in 2013. "Summerfest" in August, 2012 was the kickoff event for these special celebrations. The music, singing, and children's activities organized by both the formal and informal educational arms of the congregation, and with the assistance of the synagogue's affiliates, were attended by numerous families.[177] These programs also served as an introduction to the congregation for many new families, and by the fall of 2012 Chuck Kahalnik reported a net increase of nineteen member families. 2013 would also mark Rabbi Kurtz's twenty-five years as senior rabbi of the congregation. In honor of that occasion, in the spring of 2013 the synagogue published and distributed to its members a book authored by Rabbi Kurtz entitled *Encountering Torah: Reflections on the Weekly Portion*, a compilation of sermons delivered by the rabbi throughout his tenure at Beth El. The publication of the rabbi's book also served as a fundraising opportunity to benefit the educational programs at the synagogue.

In another well-intentioned effort to secure needed funds for operations of the synagogue, in the summer of 2012 Lisa Rosenkranz changed the name of the "Fair Share Dues" program to "Chesed Dues." It fell short of its goal. The reason, many thought, was due to the phenomenal success of the funds being raised in honor of Rabbi Kurtz's new book. By 2013, Jeffrey Goldsmith, Vice President Finance, announced that nearly $500,000 had been collected for the synagogue as a result of that project, an achievement which would provide at least $50,000 annually for the next eight years for special educational purposes. It was also announced that Richard Janger, who had overseen the North Suburban Synagogue Beth

---

177   In 2012, the Men's Club, which regularly sponsored a symposium for candidates for public office, named its programs that year in memory of Michael Simkin, the popular former Men's Club president who had passed away suddenly that year.

El Endowment Corporation (which by then had assets of close to $6 million) since its inception in 1986, would be stepping down and Ken Levin would henceforth assume that responsibility. The 65th anniversary celebration, which included the celebration of Rabbi Kurtz's 25th year at Beth El, culminated at a special congregational dinner and program, "A Night of Dreams," on April 28, 2013, chaired by Karen and Michael Kesner, Jackie and Michael Melinger, and Jenna and David Smiley. It was a beautiful and memorable affair.

As Beth El was celebrating its 65th anniversary, it was clear that the synagogue was recovering from the economic challenges of the prior five years. At its March, 2013 meeting, the Board of Directors approved an "anonymous gift" to the synagogue of over $1 million for major improvements to the Blumberg Auditorium (which, when the project was completed, was revealed to be through the generosity of Ken and Andy Saffir). The project, designed by architect Cyrus Subawalla of CSA Partners Ltd., who had become well acquainted with the synagogue through his work on the 2007 Master Plan, envisioned a floor-to-ceiling glass wall along the entire east side of the large hall, providing an expansive view of the backyard and Lake Michigan. The plan also included the construction of a large stone terrace on the exterior of the auditorium and the elimination of the auditorium's stage along the south wall, space that would be converted into a greatly needed staging area for the kitchen and catering activities.[178] Construction on this major undertaking began in May, 2013 and was completed on schedule by August of that summer;[179] it had been closely supervised by Seth Pines and Karen Kesner.

The newly renovated auditorium overlooked the English tea house, part of the original Price Estate constructed in 1911. For many years its condition had been ignored; it had deteriorated

---

[178]   Beth El's Sisterhood would once again demonstrate its generosity and importance to the congregation by donating the funds for this area and for needed kitchen improvements.

[179]   The dedicatory plaque recognizing the contribution of the Saffirs for the renovated auditorium reads, at the request of Andy Saffir, "May it be a place for many *smachot*."

and had become a storage area for the synagogue's maintenance staff. The Blumberg Auditorium renovation plan originally adopted by the Board had included the demolition of this small but architecturally significant structure. This changed when Morton and Miriam Steinberg agreed to undertake the renovation of the tea house, which occurred under the supervision of Stuart Cohen during the summer of 2014.

Beth El's new educational structure was driving the recovery of enrollment and programing at its schools. With a total enrollment of 400 students and with a fully integrated curriculum from pre-school through high school, Beth El had the largest synagogue educational system of all Conservative congregations in the Chicago area. In addition, many children in the congregation were attending the Solomon Schechter Day School and Beth El provided the largest synagogue contingent of students attending the Chicagoland Jewish High School.[180] All congregants could take pride in Beth El's achievements and continuing commitment to quality Jewish education. And in the spring of 2013, Noah Braverman, a student in the Cohen Religious School, was one of only nine North American winners of the "My Family Story" project sponsored by Beit Hatfutsot: The Museum of the Jewish People in Tel Aviv, which included a trip for him to Israel.[181]

Along with the decline in membership which had occurred over the previous years, the Ritual Committee under Vice President Richard Schlosberg had also observed a lower attendance at *Shabbat* religious services.[182] Much discussion by that committee and at meetings of the Board of Directors would occur over the next several years in an effort to encour-

---

180 In 2015, the Chicagoland Jewish High School was renamed in memory of Rochelle Zell, a former congregant of Beth El.

181 In subsequent years, Jason Garfinkel, Lila Golson, David Ayzman and Noah Hersch, all Beth El students, also won trips to Israel as part of the "My Family Story" project.

182 At the February, 2013 meeting of the Ritual Committee, it was announced that Joseph Ament, who had served as a member of that committee for over forty years, was stepping down; he was profusely thanked for his long-term dedication to the synagogue.

age attendance at these services. One idea was to hold special-ly themed services to attract different segments of the commu-nity. This gained approval and the first of these special services, organized by Jack Blumberg in conjunction with Gail Scully, Vice President Membership, and the Senior Life Committee,[183] co-chaired by Mally Rutkoff and Judy Smith, was held on July 13, 2013. The "longtime members" *Shabbat* honored all who had been members of the synagogue for at least forty years. Hundreds attended. In subsequent years, other *Shabbatot* were designated to honor members who were veterans of military service, multi-generational families at Beth El,[184] individuals who had celebrated their bar or bat mitzvah at Beth El, mem-bers over the age of seventy, and other themes.

Lisa Rosenkranz became Beth El's new president in May, 2013. At her installation ceremony, she spoke about her experiences growing up at Beth El, going to Hebrew School and celebrating her bat mitzvah at Beth El, and being in the USY group at Beth El, then revealing that all of this occurred at Beth El Synagogue in Omaha, Nebraska (from which more than a few members had relocated to the Highland Park Beth El over the years). She also put forth her agenda for the ensuing two years, including a goal of increasing membership and members' participation in syna-gogue life and a commitment to maintain Beth El's reputation as a "warm and welcoming" community. In this vein and mo-tivated by the book *Relational Judaism* by Dr. Ron Wolfson, the following January the "Practical Guide for Community Building at Beth El Programs" prepared by Rabbi Schwab was introduced to the Board.

Another innovation of President Rosenkranz was the intro-duction of an educational segment to some meetings of the

---

[183] In 2014, the Senior Life Committee began using the term "Hazak" in its name, identifying with the United Synagogue of Conservative Judaism's use of the word for "mature" Jews.

[184] That *Shabbat*, June 25, 2016, also recognized the 90th birthday of Eli Krumbein, certainly at that time the longest tenured member of Beth El. It also featured a tour of the historic Price mansion by Mort Steinberg, includ-ing a rare opportunity to visit the normally off-limits third floor "ballroom" of the mansion.

Board of Directors, beginning in August, 2013 with a session on *"Slichot"* led by Rabbi Schwab. That fall Ron Goldberg, Vice President Ritual, prepared a very useful guide for those individuals who served as *gabai* on the *bimah* during the reading of the Torah and later a similar guide for ushers was prepared. The Ritual Committee also decided to eliminate the late evening service on Erev Rosh Hashanah at the synagogue and to hold only one service that evening, thus allowing all members to join as one community at the start of the High Holy Days. At the Board meeting that August, it was also noted that attendance at the service on the second day of Rosh Hashanah at Highland Park High School had significantly declined and a discussion was held to consider also moving that service to the synagogue, but no action was taken. In October, the Gray Cultural and Learning Center hosted a book launch for *Out of Chaos: Hidden Children Remember the Holocaust*, published by Northwestern University, featuring articles by Beth El members Nicole Dreyfus Terry, Amos Turner and Edith Singer Turner.

2014 saw much activity at Beth El. In January, the synagogue sold the townhouse on Judson Avenue that it had purchased in 1983 and, after paying all expenses, realized a gain of $147,000. In February, Pam Schlosberg informed the Board that the Gray Cultural and Learning Center had earned Advanced Accreditation from the Association of Jewish Libraries, one of only fifty such institutions in the country, an outstanding achievement for the synagogue, Rachel Kamin and the Cultural and Learning Center Committee. That March, the "Big Event" was "Time Flies – A Vintage Affair," arranged by Stacy and Jeffrey Goldsmith, Irene and Gary Savine, and Barbara and Stuart Hochwert. It was a gala "supper club" celebration of Beth El's past and future and proved to be a successful event, raising over $70,000 and providing all who attended with a joyous evening. In April, the British Torah scholar Avivah Zornberg spoke at Beth El. Also that spring the Ritual Committee and Rabbi Schwab introduced "Birthdays of the Month": at one Friday night service each month, all celebrating their birthday during that month would be recognized and special refreshments would follow the service. Those efforts, along with other efforts of the Membership Committee, such as the "Welcome Baby" gift for newborns of young member families, and especially an effort by Rabbi Schwab to encourage families with children enrolled in the Steinberg Pre-School to become members of the congregation, were successful. By December, 2014, Gail Scully informed the Board that membership in the congregation stood at 1,089 families.

But the increased attendance at services and the modest increase in membership in the congregation were not reflected in the enrollment at the Miriam and Bernard H. Sokol Hebrew High School, where enrollment had dropped to seventy-eight students by September, 2014. Soon innovations were introduced to the curriculum: the study of comparative religions was offered and various field trips were undertaken, including visits to the Islamic Cultural Center in Northbrook, the Illinois Holocaust Museum in Skokie, the Ramah Day Camp in Wheeling, and the Presbyterian Church in Highland Park. Nonetheless, enrollment continued to decline.

In April, 2014, Jeffrey Goldsmith, Vice President Finance, announced that Beth El was one of only fifteen congregations in the country chosen to participate in the Harold Grinspoon Foundation program "Creating a Jewish Legacy," which would provide the synagogue with monetary incentives to have members commit to include the synagogue in their estate plans. Working with Nancy Kekst, the Ner Tamid Society, under the chairmanship of Gerald Blumberg, was organized at Beth El and within the next several years, over sixty families had made this commitment. Nonetheless, Goldsmith also noted that giving to the synagogue for most families was not necessarily a simple thing. Addressing the Board, he asked, "How do we explain the many ways to give at Beth El – B'Yachad, Chesed, Ner Tamid, naming opportunities, *Kol Nidre*, and many more; it can be very confusing." He and Kekst worked diligently on this issue, and by June of that year Kekst was able to report an increase of 9% in voluntary giving over the prior year, and the *Kol Nidre* appeal that fall exceeded $200,000, a record amount.

2014 also brought many distinguished speakers to the synagogue to teach and enlighten congregants, including Rabbi Reuven Hammer from Israel, Rabbi Gershom Sizomu of the Jewish community in Uganda, Reverend Dee Dee Coleman in honor of Martin Luther King Day, and Eitan Fishbane from the faculty of the Jewish Theological Seminary.

Events outside of Highland Park would again have a significant impact on the congregation. The Conservative movement continued to experience the challenges of a "waning" membership and steps were needed to revitalize it. Beth El, being one of the most prominent congregations in the movement, paid close attention to the efforts of the United Synagogue of Conservative Judaism (USCJ) to accomplish this. Its primary effort in 2014 was a proposal to alter the dues structure of its member congregations to a theoretically more equitable structure. Specifically, USCJ proposed to assess dues based on a synagogue's operational revenue rather than on the number of its congregants. Beth El's Board of Directors discussed the proposal at length, and even though the proposal would likely result in an increase of its annual dues to USCJ, the Board, by the close vote of twelve "yes" and eleven "no," directed President Rosenkranz to vote "for" the proposal. At the Special Meeting of the General Assembly of Kehillot of the USCJ held on March 9 and attended by more than 300 individuals in person and online, despite the vote by Beth El, the proposal was not approved.[185] At the ensuing Beth El Board of Directors meeting in April, Rosenkranz reported that as a result of the USCJ vote, Beth El's dues to USCJ for that year would be lower than anticipated and thus a "surplus" of about $3,000 existed. The Board, in a burst of generosity, immediately approved donating that amount to USCJ. But in June, after considering the various expenditures it was facing,

185 The following year, in an effort to raise needed funds, USCJ sold its headquarters building on Second Avenue in Manhattan and relocated to rental facilities at 120 Broadway, New York, New York.

the Board decided to defer that donation.[186] Finally in July, the Board approved sharing the surplus with three other needy congregations in the Chicago area.[187]

The growing incidence of terrorist activity in Israel and Europe also impacted the congregation. In June, when news of the kidnapping and murder of three Israeli teenage boys reached Beth El, Rabbi Schwab quickly called for a special gathering at the next day's *mincha* service "to stand together, grieve as a community, and pay tribute to these precious Jewish souls" and to recite special memorial prayers. Over 200 congregants attended that solemn gathering.

On June 27, 2014, President Rosenkranz sent "An Important Announcement" by email to the congregation. She informed the members that Hazzan Larry Goller would be leaving Beth El in June, 2015 at the expiration of his contract. A message from Hazzan Goller accompanied the announcement, in which he noted his meaningful time at Beth El and his desire to maintain his special relationship with its members after his departure.[188] That fall, the Ritual Committee distributed a survey among members of the congregation to ascertain their views about the role of a *hazzan* at Beth El. The information gleaned from the survey would have a positive effect on the congregation in the months to follow.

While the extraordinary events of 2014 were occurring, a myriad of other programs were taking place, many part of the annual cycle of synagogue life: the Sisterhood held Torah Fund classes and in July at the Women's League national convention, it received the coveted Emerald Award for achievement in educational programming and community service; the Men's Club[189] hosted its

---

[186] It was at this meeting that it was duly noted that Beth El's neighboring Reform congregation in Highland Park, B'nai Torah, had closed, primarily due to its inability to repay excessive borrowings.

[187] The recipients of the surplus were the Sons of Abraham Synagogue in Lafayette, Indiana, the Central Synagogue of Chicago, and the Ner Tamid Ezra Habonim Egalitarian Minyan in West Rogers Park, Chicago.

[188] Hazzan Goller soon thereafter became a certified chaplain and in 2017 became hazzan at Shelter Rock Jewish Center in Roslyn, New York.

[189] In February, 2014, Ernie Smolen was recognized by the Midwest Region of Men's Clubs as the Man of the Year, a significant honor. Sadly, he passed away in 2017.

weekly Bagels for Your Brains sessions on Sunday mornings; Ali Drumm organized numerous informal educational programs, including "Jeans and Jammies" and women's Rosh Chodesh groups; Rabbi Kurtz and Samantha Isenstein visited Beth El's college students at the University of Illinois; a new Levenfeld Family Sukkah, expertly designed by Greg Pestine (certified 100% kosher by Rabbi Kurtz) and erected on the new terrace of the Blumberg Auditorium, was ready for Sukkot; the Social Action Committee led by Jackie Kotte-Wolle sponsored the annual Thanksgiving Mitzvah project to provide food for needy families in Lake County; Beth El's USY group, still the largest chapter in its region, held numerous programs throughout the year, most notably its annual Turkey Dance on Thanksgiving weekend; the Gertrude Lederman Adult Education programs enrolled almost 350 students during the year; and once again Larry Goldstein made the arrangements for congregants to lead the summertime *Shabbat* services, with Ron Goldberg, Vice President Ritual, reporting to the Board: "Larry just gets it done, with no drama!" And, of course, the Board of Directors approved additional necessary repairs to the roof, this time over the Field Family Sanctuary.

In February 2015, the Men's Club under president Robert Freeman held its first annual Caveman Dinner (meat dishes, finger foods, no silverware, but "the usual libations"). That same month, Aaron Krumbein was recognized as Man of the Year by the Midwest Region of the Federation of Jewish Men's Club. In March, the spring fundraising event was a concert by Peter Himmelman, the award-winning musician and son-in-law of Bob Dylan. Over 300 people attended the event, which included a silent auction. It was chaired by Diane and Loren Weil, Michelle Gooze-Miller and Adam Miller, with Felissa Kreindler as ad book chair and with the always capable assistance of Nancy Kekst. At the meeting of the Board of Directors that month, Samantha Isenstein, Youth Community Director, and Joey Spellberg, USY President, presented an in-depth report on the numerous activities of the Beth El chapter of USY and other youth activities.

In one of her last official acts as president, Lisa Rosenkranz in May, 2015 distributed to the congregation a report entitled "A Dynamic New Educational Pathway." Developed by a task force led by Rabbis Kurtz and Schwab and including Alicia Gejman, Ali Drumm and the two Vice Presidents Education, Tracey Hendler and Pam Schlosberg, the report created an education structure for the Cohen Religious School with more flexible hours for its students yet maintaining its high standards of education with a core curriculum of Hebrew language, Torah, history, and weekly family *Shabbat* services. The new program was instituted in the fall of 2015.

Richard Schlosberg assumed the presidency of Beth El in May, 2015. At his first Board meeting, he emphasized the responsibility of all directors and trustees to uphold the reputation for excellence in all aspects of synagogue life which Beth El had earned over the past years.[190] Yet he also noted the importance of innovation in planning for the future of the synagogue. At the same meeting, Larry Silberman, Treasurer, announced that Abe Rotbart had been hired as a part-time controller to assist the Executive Director with accounting matters, a position which would soon become full-time. Silberman also reported that the synagogue's long-term debt of $750,000 had been successfully refinanced at advantageous terms with BMO Harris Bank in Chicago.

On the second day of Shavuot in May, 2015, which coincided with Memorial Day, Larry Goller was honored at religious services. More than 600 people gathered in the Field Family Sanctuary that morning as Hazzan Goller said goodbye to the congregation he had served for seventeen years, thanking the congregation for allowing him to serve as a teacher and for the opportunity to learn from his students and from his colleagues

190 In this vein, during the summer of 2015 the Rissman Family Kol Ami Museum featured an exhibit entitled "The Birnbaums at Beth El: 60 Years of Art and Soul," honoring the work of Marge and Leonard Birnbaum and their commitment to the synagogue for six decades.

Rabbis Kurtz and Schwab.[191]

After an extensive search by a committee chaired by Larry Pachter, the Board of Directors in April, 2015 approved bringing Hazzan Benjamin A. Tisser to Beth El from B'nai Torah Congregation in Boca Raton, Florida. Hazzan Tisser, a young and dynamic musician with a strong Judaic background, grew up in California and was awarded a Masters of Sacred Music by the H. L. Miller Cantorial School of the Jewish Theological Seminary in 2013. He and his wife, Sarah, and their two children moved to Highland Park, into the Judson Avenue residence of the synagogue, during the summer of 2015. Mark Mosk chaired a committee to assist the Tisser family's transition to life in their new community. Hazzan Tisser's first *Shabbat* as hazzan of the congregation was on August 8, 2015.

In October, 2015, Chuck Kahalnik announced his departure as Executive Director of the synagogue effective the following June. Lisa Rosenkrantz soon chaired the Executive Director Position Strategy Committee to evaluate the current needs and criteria for that position, and subsequently Audra Kaplan was asked to chair a search committee for a new executive director. Soon, the committee recommended Jeffrey Baden, and he assumed his responsibilities as the new executive director in July, 2016. Baden had held leadership roles in the Jewish Community Centers of both Cincinnati, Ohio and Ann Arbor, Michigan.[192] Prior to his departure,[193] Kahalnik and Richard Zelin, Vice President Administration, conducted a total review of the security needs and procedures at Beth El. Undertaken in conjunction with the Highland Park Police Department and the Department of Homeland Security, one recommendation of

191   That service also recognized the 70th anniversary of the end of World War II, and a special *aliyah* was given to Leonard Sherman, who had served three years in the American armed forces in the South Pacific during the war and later as a volunteer in Israel's Etzioni Brigade defending Jerusalem during Israel's War of Independence.

192   Baden's spouse, Rabbi Ilana Greenfield Baden, conveniently was serving as Senior Associate Rabbi at Temple Chai in Long Grove, Illinois at the time.

193   After his departure, Kahalnik would continue to teach in the Cohen Religious School and the Sokol Hebrew High School.

the review, in addition to continuing to provide armed security guards during school hours and other times of large gatherings, was the installation of chain link fencing and gates on the north and south sides of the synagogue building to deter uninvited access to the synagogue's backyard. This was duly approved by the Board in January, 2016 and the fencing was promptly installed.

Also that fall, Marla Grossberg chaired a subcommittee of the Ritual Committee to structure policies and practices for a family observing *shiva*, so that the congregation could properly provide resources and support to the mourners. And that winter, Rabbi Schwab, who had served the synagogue for more than ten years, availed himself of a three-month sabbatical with his family on an RV road trip to the southwest United States, for the purpose, in his words, to "refresh, re-charge and to... strengthen my ability as a rabbi to contribute to our community...."

In December, 2015, at the United Synagogue Youth International Convention in Baltimore, attended by fifteen Beth El USYers, the Beth El chapter once again received the well-deserved award for making the highest contribution of any U.S. chapter to the USY Tikkun Olam Fund. At the Board meeting that month, Larry Silberman announced that the synagogue was "financially strong" but that it was important to expand "revenue streams." That same month a Hanukkah Disco Party for the young families of the congregation was a smashing success with over 400 children and adults in attendance.

Continuing its tradition of providing insightful and relevant resources, Beth El hosted many well-known speakers in 2015, including Dr. Donniel Hartman from Jerusalem, Dr. Arnold Eisen, Chancellor of the Jewish Theological Seminary, Dr. Daniel Gordis of Shalem College in Jerusalem, Professor Benjamin Gampel, also from the Seminary, and Rabbi Jonathan Wittenberg, Senior Rabbi of Masorti Judaism in the United Kingdom.

In the spring of 2016, Tovah Goodman was hired as the new Youth Community Director. Not only experienced working with Jewish youth of different ages, including at summer camps and on Birthright trips to Israel, she also was extremely talented in Jewish music. Also that spring, in a forward-looking action, President Schlosberg appointed a Long Range Strategic Planning Committee, co-chaired by Lisa Rosenkranz and Roberta Kwall, to examine polices of the synagogue dealing with new issues likely to be faced in the future.

With the arrival of Hazzan Tisser the congregation began to experience a new surge in exciting musical programing and also some innovation at religious services, particularly on the High Holidays. One of the first programs, held over the weekend of January 22-23, 2016, was an amazing a cappella concert featuring groups from five universities. It was a sold out, standing-room-only event attended by over 700 people who filled the Field Family Sanctuary and the Paset Lounge. In the months following, the hazzan arranged first for a "Night in the Catskills" concert featuring Cantor Herschel Fox and Beth El's own Tovah Goodman and Sarah Tenner, and then "Jazz on the Lake" with noted musician Howard Levy. For the High Holidays, Hazzan Tisser retained Sid Engel, a well-known music arranger, to direct the professional choir in the Field Family Sanctuary, and he invited several young members of the Youth Community to join him in beautifully chanting certain prayers.[194]

Caron Knopoff, who had succeeded in her efforts to make significant improvements to the Steinberg Pre-School, retired as its director in 2016. A search committee headed by Larry Pachter recommended Karee Bilsky, a recognized authority in the field of early childhood education, then serving as Director of Gan Ami Early Childhood Center at the Samson Family JCC in Milwaukee. The Board of Directors quickly approved her as the new Pre-School director and she began her duties in the summer of 2016. By that time, the Steinberg Pre-School had become the "hot" location among parents in the community for pre-school age children. Enrollment grew in the fall of 2016

---

[194] During the High Holidays of 2015 and 2016, these students included Elena Gross, Sarah Tenner, Emily Zimmerman, Rebecca Halfin, and Rachel Hochberg.

to 200, with waiting lists for certain ages. At 9:00 a.m. each weekday morning, the synagogue parking lot literally was filled with SUVs and minivans as parents escorted their children into the Beth El school building to begin their Jewish education, the continuation of a Beth El tradition of seventy years.

As the 2015-2016 fiscal year came to a close in July, Larry Silberman was once again able to report that Beth El was in a strong financial position with close to a $1 million balance in its operating fund and with total assets in excess of $13 million. He stated: the "synagogue on the whole has had another success-ful year, financially." In September, at the urging of President Schlosberg, the synagogue by-laws were amended to create the new position of Vice President Programming, which would have responsibility essentially overall non-religious activities, in-cluding Social Action and HAZAK Senior Life. The first person to fill this position was Melissa Halperin, but only unofficially until the next election of officers in the spring of 2017, at which time Jackie Melinger was chosen to serve in that position and Halper-in assumed the responsibilities of Vice President Membership. In another adjustment of responsibilities, Rabbi Schwab took upon himself, as of July, 2016, the supervision of all educational programming at the synagogue. As Kim Ephraim, Vice President Education, noted, there was work to be done in this area: while the Steinberg Pre-School was experiencing a resurgence, the Cohen Religious School enrollment was flat, and enrollment in the Sokol High School continued to decline. By the fall of 2017, only forty students were enrolled in the High School program.

Yet the challenges of operating and maintaining the large congregation, its myriad of educational and cultural programs and its facilities continued. By this time, including the facul-ty of its schools and its educational personnel, the clergy, the administrative staff, the custodial staff and others, almost ninety people were employed by the synagogue. Annual dues, which by 2015 had reached $3,060 per family, were sufficient to cover only about one-half of the synagogue's annual bud-get. The need to raise annually the funds to provide the high level of programing for which Beth El had become known was a constant challenge facing the Board of Directors.[195] Continuing efforts to meet this challenge, the "Big Event" in the spring of 2016 was a successful Mediterranean Cabaret featuring a concert by Basya Schechter and her band, Pharaoh's Daughter; 200 people attended and $53,000 was raised.

For some time discussions had been underway focusing on two areas of the synagogue for physical improvement: the corridor around the perimeter of the Field Family Sanctuary and the Sager Bet HaMidrash. Audra Kaplan, Vice President Administration, reported on these undertakings as early as 2013, and the following spring architect Cyrus Subawalla was again retained to prepare plans for these projects. Both areas, including the memorial alcove at the entry to the Sager Bet HaMidrash and the adjacent central restrooms, had been in almost constant use since construction of the sanctuary building fifty years earlier. The small sanctuary, used twice every day for the *minyan* and other activities, had not been renovated for many years. Much of the impetus for this project was generated by the Cultural and Learning Center Committee which had responsibility for the Rissman Kol Ami Collection. Seeking enlarged and improved facilities for the display of the museum's growing assemblage of Judaic art and ritual treasures and for new contemporary exhibitions, the committee, most prominently Marla Hand and Pam Schlosberg,[196] sought to have the corridor renovated to accommodate the displays and new display cases.

Numerous meetings of the House Committee, the Cultural and Learning Center Committee and others took place over several years. Finally, with a generous donation from the Estate of

---

195   One indication of the maturity of the congregation at this time was the fact that the weekly *yahrtzeit* list published in the *Shabbat* bulletin often numbered eighty or ninety names and occasionally exceeded 100 names.

196   In 2015, Pam Schlosberg, who served as Vice President Education, received the distinct honor of being granted the Valued Volunteer Award by the Central Great Lakes Region of Women's League for Conservative Judaism. That May she also graciously resigned as Vice President Education so that her husband, Richard, could serve as president without his spouse also serving on the Executive Committee. She soon assumed the chair of the Cultural and Learning Center Committee.

Maurice and Hynda Gamze, in June, 2016 the sanctuary building was closed off entirely from the rest of the synagogue facilities as the corridor around the sanctuary was essentially reconstructed in what was called the West Wing Project; the following year it was dedicated as the Gamze Gallery.[197] Also instrumental in enabling this project to be undertaken were generous gifts from Mark and Mae Spitz, Skip and Lynn Schrayer, and the family of the late Howard Lidov, who dedicated the expanded memorial alcove in memory of that former president of Beth El. Work on the West Wing Project was supervised by Richard Zelin, Vice President Administration, and Seth Pines of the House Committee and was completed on schedule just before Rosh Hashanah that fall.[198] All religious services during the summer of 2016 were held in the newly renovated Blumberg Auditorium with beautiful views over Lake Michigan, a reminder of the reason the Price Estate had been named "Bonita Vista."

The second phase of the renovation project took place later in the winter and spring of 2017: the Sager Bet HaMidrash[199] was totally renovated with another major gift from the Sisterhood. Nissah Mattenson and the grandchildren of Ben and Florence Sager also assisted in this endeavor. The work included the restoration of the original design of the Price Estate sun parlor at its east end and the installation of a new *aron kodesh* and reading table, and eventually a new *ner tamid*, all designed by architect/designer Amy Reichert.[200] The renovated Sager Beit HaMidrash was ready for use by Passover in the spring of

---

[197] Since normal interior access from the Blumberg Auditorium to the other facilities was restricted, accommodations were made for those familiar with the layout of the various Beth El structures to have interior access through the basement of the Price mansion and via the school building.

[198] In November, 2016, Jeff Baden informed the Board that repairs to the roof over the newly completed West Wing Project were urgently needed, another Beth El tradition.

[199] In connection with this work, the spelling of this facility was altered to read variously "Beit HaMidrash" or just "Beit Midrash."

[200] Reichert also assisted in the design of the new custom-made exhibition cases installed for the displays of the Rissman Kol Ami Collection in the new Gamze Gallery.

2017. Simultaneously, Robert Footlik, volunteering totally on his own, completed the organization of and improvement to the extensive basement of the mansion building, installing new lighting fixtures, shelving and numerous safety features. This was an urgently needed undertaking for an area very few congregants would ever view.

As part of the effort to improve communication between the synagogue and its members, to increase membership in the congregation, and generally to support and sustain its mission, a new Communications Committee was formed in October, 2016 under the leadership of Pam Schlosberg and with the professional assistance of Nancy Kekst. Its initial focus was on improving and "refreshing" Beth El's "brand." As a result, the synagogue would "update" its color palette, improve its website, and adopt a new typeface for the Beth El logo, making it less "script" in appearance and projecting a "bold" image. It was immediately implemented, but not without some negative reactions.

The fall of 2016 saw the revitalization of the Junior Congregation, a *Shabbat* service for fifth and sixth grade children. This was accomplished through the efforts of Rabbi Schwab, the Director of Formal Education Alicia Gejman, and Hazzan Barbara Barnett of the Cohen Religious School faculty. Also that fall, the Ritual Committee under Vice President Ritual David Shapiro reaffirmed the synagogue's policy that interfaith life-cycle events would not be announced from the *bimah* during religious services, but that life-cycle events of Jewish partners, regardless of sexual orientation or gender identity, would be announced at the request of the families.

Continuing its tradition of having prominent and relevant speakers address the congregation on important issues, in January, 2017, Beth El was the site for the program entitled "Left vs. Right: The Battle for Israe's Soul," featuring a lively dialogue between Jonathan Tobin of *Commentary* magazine and J. J. Goldberg of the *Forward*. It was moderated by Rabbi Kurtz and Rabbi Wendi Geffen of North Shore Congregation Israel, the co-sponsor of the event. Later in the year, Rabbi Bradley

Shavit Arston, Dean of the Ziegler School of Rabbinic Studies at the American Jewish University in California, would serve as the Robbin Scholar in Residence.

On February 14, 2017, in an email "Note from the Beth El President," Richard Schlosberg informed the congregation that he was facing "various medical challenges" and that he would be absent from the synagogue for an undetermined interval. He requested all to respect his privacy and to refrain from telephone calls and visits. During the remaining three months of his term, Larry Pachter, Secretary, ably filled in to chair the meetings of the Board of Directors. Happily, Schlosberg was able to resume attendance at synagogue events during the summer of 2017.

Numerous events were planned for the year-long celebration in 2017 in honor of Rabbi Schwab's thirteenth "bar mitzvah" anniversary at Beth El: a special Mitzvah Day, a special *Shabbat*, and a community-wide party featuring activities for all ages and entertainment by singer Naomi Less. Also, a new Family Engagement Fund was established. Focusing on the families with children enrolled in the Steinberg Pre-School, the purpose of this effort was to help ensure that Beth El would become the most dynamic young family synagogue community on the North Shore.

Richard Zelin became Beth El's thirty-third president in May, 2017. Experienced professionally in Jewish community leadership, at his installation he also noted his acquired knowledge of building construction during his recent stint as Vice President Administration. Recognizing the significant achievements by the synagogue since its founding, and the reputation for excellence it had acquired and maintained, he announced that his mission for the future "is that we can go from being very good to great. Not perfect. But great!"

At the first Board meeting of Zelin's term as president, in June, 2017, an announcement was made that as part of its 70th anniversary celebration the congregation would undertake a major capital and endowment campaign seeking to increase the synagogue's endowment by $1.8 million through the establishment of the Senior Rabbinic Chair in honor of Rabbi Kurtz. The new campaign, entitled "Vision 70: 70th Anniversary Campaign for North Suburban Synagogue Beth El," would be chaired by Karen Kesner, Larry Pachter and Stuart Hochwert. It would also seek to secure funds to undertake renovations to increase physical access within the synagogue and also funds to create "compelling, cutting-edge educational and cultural programs...to attract and appeal to families in every age range." Within eight months, before the public phase of the Campaign had even commenced, the Campaign had secured pledges in excess of $2 million.[201] (The 70th Anniversary Campaign was officially approved by the Board of Directors in March, 2018.) Meanwhile, plans for the 70th anniversary celebration were advancing under the leadership of Annette and Gerald Blumberg, Wendy and Steve Abrams, and Jenna and David Smiley. A detailed schedule of the many events planned throughout the year was distributed to each congregant at High Holiday services in 2017. Included in the plans were several reunions (past members of USY/BEANS, Beth El bar and bat mitzvah celebrants, etc.), concerts, special speakers, and such diverse events as unique cooking classes (including one led by Hazzan Tisser!), a song-writing contest, and an adult "March of the Living" mission to Poland and Israel to be led by Rabbi Kurtz, which would also celebrate Israel's 70th Anniversary.

In June, 2017, Nancy Kekst, who had been successful over the past years in development and communications at the synagogue, announced she was leaving Beth El to start her own consulting firm.[202] That summer, Andrew Brown, chairman of the committee to find a new Development Director, recommended hiring Judy Berkeley, who joined Beth El in September. Shortly thereafter, Abby Lasky joined the synagogue

---

201 Ken Levin also advised the Board that the Endowment Corporation had decided to switch investment funds from the JUF Pooled Fund to a fund under the direction of Mesirow Financial.

202 One of Kekst's first clients was Beth El, which asked her to serve as a consultant to its new capital and endowment campaign.

as the new Marketing/Communications Director.[203] In August, with the critical assistance of Phil Feitelberg, a Senior Rabbinic Gallery displaying photographs of all five of Beth El's senior rabbis was established near the Sager Beit HaMidrash. It was the first time in the synagogue's history that those who had served in that essential role received permanent recognition.[204] And in September, the first exhibit in the newly dedicated Gamze Gallery opened: "Sacred Space: Wrapped in Spirituality" by Jane Cooperman and Karen Bieber, a beautiful display of special *talitot*.

At Rosh Hashanah services in the fall of 2017, Hazzan Tisser made another innovative presentation: a unique rendering of the Hallelujah prayer at *musaf* in the melody of the same name composed by the recently deceased poet and songwriter Leonard Cohen. On Simchat Torah, David Shapiro read the concluding paragraphs of the Torah for the twenty-fifth consecutive year and then was honored as the *Chatan Torah*. At that service, Marla Hand received the honor of *Kol Ha Nearim* and in recognition of his thirty years at Beth El, Rabbi Kurtz was honored as *Chatan B'reisheet*.[205]

To kick-off the 70th anniversary celebration, the congregation was invited to a special family celebration in the Blumberg Auditorium in October, 2017 featuring special T-shirts for all, music, jugglers, dance contests, and a sumptuous luncheon. A photograph of the hundreds of congregants in attendance was taken in the Field Family Sanctuary. Also that October, on *Shabbat Parshat Bereshit*, the congregation began using the new *Siddur Lev Shalem for Shabbat and Festivals*,[206] described by

---

203   One of Lasky's many achievements was the transformation, within a few months, of the weekly *Shabbat* bulletin from a simple handout to the "Shabbat Insider," a colorful and informative publication.

204   The five were Rabbis Maurice I. Kliers, Philip L. Lipis, Samuel H. Dresner, William H. Lebeau and Vernon H. Kurtz.

205   In another recognition of Rabbi Kurtz's tenure at Beth El, in December the Men's Club honored him with its Keeper of the Flame Award at a "roast and toast" dinner chaired by Daryl Temkin.

206   Earlier in the year, on Tishah B'Av, the congregation began using the new edition of *Siddur Tishah B'Av*, also published by the Rabbinical Assembly.

Rabbi Kurtz as a *siddur* that "offers multiple pathways into the Jewish prayer experience..., a highly readable translation, and [it] is a prayer book for both home and the synagogue." In preparation for its introduction, Hazzan Tisser had led a series of sessions over the prior months to acquaint the congregation with the new prayer book. As with *Mahzor Lev Shalem* introduced seven years earlier for the High Holy Days, the practice of the congregation was to follow the more traditional presentation of the prayers. *Siddur Sim Shalom*, in use at the synagogue since 1986, continued to be used for weekday services.

In November, another popular concert was organized by Hazzan Tisser and the Music Committee chaired by Jeffrey Goldsmith to celebrate both the 70th anniversary of Beth El and the 70th anniversary of the State of Israel: a performance by the well-known Israeli musical artist Bat Ella. Almost 400 congregants filled the Field Family Sanctuary to hear a mixture of modern and "old time" Israeli music; the audience was literally dancing in the aisles, enthusiastically led by Rabbi Kurtz and President Zelin![207]

Soon, President Zelin appointed another new committee: the Committee on Accessibility and Inclusion of People with Disabilities. Its co-chairs were Rabbi Schwab, Rachel Ferber and Audra Kaplan. Although the synagogue was in full compliance with the Americans with Disabilities Act, many felt that new accommodations could be instituted, such as electric doors, wheelchair-accessible ramps and lifts to the *bimah* in the Field Family Sanctuary and the Zell Activity Room. The Committee's primary goal was to allow people with disabilities and their families to participate comfortably and fully at Beth El.[208] Rabbi Schwab would soon become very committed to this

---

[207] Bat Ella was accompanied by a seven-piece band, including Beth El's own Fran Sherman on violin. The program was one of the first from the synagogue to be live-streamed on the Internet.

[208] In November, 2017, Stacy Daybrook, coordinator of the Cal and Lana Eisenberg Halomdim Program, an important synagogue program serving children with learning disabilities, was the recipient of the Hartman Foundation Educator of the Year Award for her work at the Arie Crown Hebrew Day School in Skokie.

undertaking.[209] In the fall of 2017, after portions of the country were devastated by Hurricanes Harvey, Irma and Maria, Rabbi Schwab also quickly led efforts to provide relief to the Jewish communities in Houston and Puerto Rico which bore the brunt of those storms. Toward the end of the year, Scott Forrester, Treasurer, announced that the name of the Budget Committee had been changed to the Finance Committee to better reflect its overall responsibility and happily pointed out that for the prior fiscal year, revenues exceeded the budget by $176,000, due primarily to the Circle of Life food service and the Steinberg Pre-School tuitions. It was an encouraging note on which to greet Beth El's 70th anniversary.

By now many congregants anticipated that Vernon Kurtz, who had served as senior rabbi at Beth El for close to thirty years and who had enriched the congregation during those three decades with his scholarship and serious concern for Judaism and *halacha*, would soon embark upon a new and less demanding pathway in his accomplished career. That anticipation was answered on November 28, 2017 when the congregation received by email "An Important Message from President Richard Zelin." Zelin related the news that Rabbi Kurtz had decided to retire as senior rabbi at Beth El effective June 30, 2019. He continued:

> Rabbi Kurtz has led us with compassion, deep knowledge, and a steady guiding hand....His knowledge of Jewish law as well as his understanding of the background and experiences of our congregational family is deep and broad. He has been a part of our families, and we have become part of his....NSSBE is the strong, vibrant congregation it is today in great measure because of his leadership. (He) will be greatly missed.

Zelin outlined the procedure that would be followed to provide a successor to Rabbi Kurtz. A Transition Committee chaired

---

209 Subsequently, Rabbi Schwab was named co-chair of the Jewish United Fund Synagogue Federation Commission, and he envisioned synagogue inclusion and accessibility as its main goal.

by Larry Pachter had already been appointed by the previous president, Richard Schlosberg. Being in the unprecedented position of having a second rabbi who had served the congregation so admirably over the past fourteen years, that committee had consulted with both the United Synagogue of Conservative Judaism and the Rabbinical Assembly as to the appropriate approach to selecting a new senior rabbi. The Committee held formal discussions with Rabbi Schwab "regarding his perspectives and approaches to being our senior rabbi." Following these discussions, which also included a broad section of the synagogue leadership, a recommendation was made to the Executive Committee, which in turn made a recommendation to the Board of Directors. On December 14, in an historic meeting,[210] the Board unanimously approved the selection of Michael Schwab to become Beth El's new senior rabbi in July, 2019. Rabbi Schwab, a graduate of Rutgers University, had been ordained by the Jewish Theological Seminary in 2004 and had spent several years studying in Israel. After almost fourteen years of service at Beth El, he was extremely active in the Chicago Jewish community, serving on the Board of Directors of the Solomon Schetcher Day School, on the Executive Committee of the Chicago Board of Rabbis, as a scholar for Jewish Values Online, and as a member of Northwestern University's Kellogg's Jewish Leaders Circle. Within five months, the Board approved purchasing the home at 771 Judson Avenue for the expanded Schwab family, which now included the rabbi and Erica's four children.

Although Rabbi Kurtz would remain the senior rabbi of Beth El for another eighteen months, in actuality he would be active only until the end of 2018 due to his scheduled sabbatical and accrued vacation time. He and Bryna planned to move to their apartment on Ein Gedi Street in Jerusalem, fulfilling the Zionist dream of living in Eretz Yisrael.[211] To assure that the congre-

---

210 A record number of directors and trustees, including twelve past presidents, attended the first meeting of directors in thirty years to select a senior rabbi.

211 Although moving to Israel, Rabbi Kurtz planned to continue his contacts with Beth El as Rabbi Emeritus and the synagogue would continue to provide minimum benefits, such as office space when he would visit the North Shore.

gation would have sufficient rabbinical support during Rabbi Kurtz's sabbatical, the Board also approved the establishment of a search committee to find an assistant rabbi to begin service at Beth El in the summer of 2018. By the following April, the Board approved the recommendation of that committee chaired by Jeff Kopin to bring Alex Freedman, Associate Rabbi of Temple Emanu-El in Closter, New Jersey, to Beth El. Rabbi Freedman was ordained by the Jewish Theological Seminary in 2013 and was a recipient of a Wexner Graduate Fellowship. He, his wife Laura and their family were expected to join the Beth El community in July.

As 2017 came to a close, Costica Mihailescu, a "dear friend" who had served as Facilities Director for more than seventeen years, announced his retirement to return to his native Romania. Within a few months, Jeff Baden announced that John Patrascu had been appointed the synagogue's new Facilities Manager. 2017 ended with exciting news for Beth El's USY chapter, as Sawyer Goldsmith was elected USY International Religion/Education Vice President at the USY International Conventional held that December in Chicago.[212] In the week prior to the convention, with almost eighty teens from New York, Israel and Europe being hosted by Beth El families, *Shabbat* services on December 23, 2017 were led entirely by members of Beth El USY.[213]

Many significant events crowded the synagogue's calendar in the first months of 2018. The year began with another musical sensation arranged by Hazzan Tisser: Ilu Finu – The Jewish Collegiate A Cappella Songwriting Competition Finale Concert and Awards Ceremony.[214] Shortly thereafter, at the invitation of

---

[212] Soon after the election, Sawyer, a student at the Rochelle Zell Jewish High School, was the subject of an article in *The Times of Israel* as the first transgender USYer to be elected to the USY International Board.

[213] Participants included: Davida Goller, Helen Spellberg, Emma Halfin, Sawyer Goldsmith, Ilana Greenstein, Gabriella Cooperman and Jordan Behn.

[214] In preparation for the concert, the Cultural and Learning Center prepared an exceptional exhibition of "70 Years of Music at Beth El," featuring numerous archival artifacts and biographies of all nine individuals who since 1948 had served the congregation as a full-time *hazzan*.

Masorti Olami, the hazzan had the honor of teaching and singing at Maayane Or, the Masorti Congregation in Nice, France. In February, the Congregation's Communications Committee went "live" with a newly-designed and interactive website for the congregation and the Men's Club facilitated a new easier-to-use Wi-Fi system at the synagogue.[215]

The educational sphere of the synagogue was also very active. In March, over 140 congregants participated in the second annual "Knead a Night Out," a community *challah* bake to benefit the Cohen Religious School, advertised as a "BYOA Affair" (Bring Your Own Apron). Early in 2018, two members of the Steinberg Pre-School faculty, Cori Katz and Sara Chupack, enrolled in JECELI, the Jewish Early Childhood Education Leadership Institute, a joint effort of the Jewish Theological Seminary and the Hebrew Union College, in consultation with the Bank Street College of Education. Its mission was to promote the leadership skills of highly qualified educators within the context of core Jewish values.[216] Alicia Gejman, the Director of Formal Education, was also giving serious thought to the educational programs of the Sokol High School, whose enrollment remained flat. In January, she reported to the Board that discussions had commenced among educators from four Conservative congregations in the area[217] about the possible establishment of a new Conservative community high school program, and those conversations continued into the spring. Also that month, in a distinct honor for the congregation, both Alicia Gejman and the Director of Informal Education, Ali Drumm, became board members of the distinguished Jewish Educators Assembly.

In February, continuing an almost annual tradition, the Board approved the replacement of the roof over the Zell Activity Room. At the same time, Seth Pines of the House Committee,

---

215   In March, the Men's Club recognized Richard Small as its Man of the Year and honored Emma Halfin, Beth El's USY president, as Youth of the Year.

216   Beth El's own Karen Benson served as one of the mentors in this critically acclaimed program.

217   The four synagogues were Moriah Congregation, Congregation B'nai Tikvah, Congregation Beth Shalom and North Suburban Synagogue Beth El.

now called the Facilities Committee, announced that a survey of the different roofs at the synagogue was being undertaken to determine a method of minimizing future roofing problems. The Facilities Committee also approved replacing the badly deteriorated Welsh tile floor on the rear portico and terraces of the Price mansion with stone pavers, a project made possible by the generosity of Skip and Lynn Schrayer. The work was completed by spring.

Throughout the winter, Rod Slutsky with assistance from Jack Blumberg, Debbie Fox and Mary Channon, planned for a reunion of every person who had celebrated a bar or bat mitzvah at Beth El, or who had completed confirmation classes during the first years of the congregation's existence. It was scheduled for May, another special event to celebrate the synagogue's 70th anniversary. Merely compiling the names of these individuals, estimated to be approximately 4,000, was an overwhelming task. Fortunately, by March, Kathy Stinson, Beth El's Events and Operations Manager, was able to compile a list of more than 3,000 individuals for the reunion. It promised to be a festive *Shabbat* experience.

Also in March, Rabbi Zev Eleff, Chief Academic Officer of the Hebrew Theological College, spoke on the history of the Conservative movement in the Chicago area, the first of several distinguished scholars scheduled to speak at the synagogue during the year. Others included Dr. Aron Zelin of the Washington Institute for Near East Policy (and the son of President Zelin); Dr. Shuly Rubin Schwartz from the Jewish Theological Seminary; and Dr. Claire Sufrin of Northwestern University. In April, under co-presidents Mary Ellen Bowers, Rachel Ferber and Karen Weiss, Sisterhood hosted the Spring Conference of the Central Great Lakes Region of Women's League for Conservative Judaism. Over 165 participants from the Midwest gathered at Beth El for friendship, worship, workshops and educational sessions.

The culminating event of the year-long commemoration of the congregation's 70th Anniversary and Israel's 70th Anniversary was a gala celebration scheduled for the weekend of November 2-4, 2018. Chaired by Pearl and Joel Kagan, Wendy and Steve Abrams, and Jenna and David Smiley, the event would feature Dr. David Golinkin of the Schechter Institute in Jerusalem and would honor Vernon and Bryna Kurtz on their thirtieth anniversary at Beth El as they prepare to depart the community. But as the congregation looked forward to those events, it was reminded once again that changes occur at Beth El. Along with the impending retirement of Rabbi Kurtz, other transitions would soon impact the congregation. Both Tovah Goodman, the Youth Community Director, and Karee Bilsky, the Pre-School Director, announced they would be leaving Beth El in June. Efforts led by Rebecca Jacobson and Sara Block were quickly undertaken to bring new leadership for those critical positions to the congregation. Within a few weeks, the synagogue announced that Kory Goldenberg, an experienced and committed early childhood professional, would become the director of the Steinberg Pre-School in July. And sadly, within one week in May, 2018, past presidents Richard Janger and Alan Rutkoff both passed away; their respective contributions to the synagogue and the greater community were solemnly recognized at their funerals held in the Field Family Sanctuary.

Having overcome the financial vicissitudes of the prior decade, Beth El's leadership envisioned the future with confidence. Notwithstanding a continued decline in membership to 1,030 families at the beginning of 2018, the Board of Directors in April approved a budget for the coming year of $4.7 million and increased dues for the great majority of families to $3,330. Soon the congregation would celebrate its seventy years of providing the North Shore with a special place to worship, learn and engage in meaningful social gatherings. Although anticipating major changes in its professional leadership, the congregation knew, in the spirit of the late Eli Field, that the Torah would still be read at Beth El.

VIII. THE FUTURE

More than seven decades had passed since a handful of families joined together to establish a Conservative congregation on the North Shore. Strengthened and nurtured over time by strong lay leadership and exceptional rabbinic and professional leaders, North Suburban Synagogue Beth El has become one of the leading Conservative synagogues in America, creating an impact on Conservative Judaism and Jewish and secular institutions not only on the North Shore but far beyond its own community.[218] By now, the dream of the congregation's founders, to build a synagogue which would serve their children and their children's children, had become a reality. A new generation of leaders had renewed the dream to maintain and enhance the traditions of the Jewish people and its ties to the State of Israel. In the words of Rabbi Vernon Kurtz, soon to be Rabbi Emeritus of the synagogue, "Rabbi Schwab [and I] have worked together very closely in a community which cares deeply about Jewish tradition, Jewish law, the Jewish people, [and] the State of Israel....I know that Rabbi Schwab's leadership in the future will take this community from strength to strength...as we plan a bright future for North Suburban Synagogue Beth El." Having overcome unforeseen challenges throughout its history, Beth El was well poised to face new challenges and to dream new dreams that will lead the congregation in that future.

---

[218] In addition to the many lay leaders of Jewish organizations locally, nationally and abroad, Beth El and its clergy inspired many of its young people to embark on a career in the rabbinate. Among these are Rabbis Charles Feinberg, Howard Gorin, Fred Margulies, David Ebstein, Brad Hirschfield, Jonathan Rosenblum, Matthew Field, Daniel Millner, William Hamilton, Lee Buckman, Ora Simon Schnitzer, Matthew Shapiro and Nolan Lebovitz.

APPENDIX

Presidents

Arnold P. Natenberg	1947-1950
Harold R. Blumberg	1950-1954
Edward M. Glazier	1954-1957
Albert H. Dolin	1957-1960
Eli Field	1960-1963
Bernard H. Sokol	1963-1965
Max Applebaum	1965-1967
Benjamin W. Sager	1967-1969
Harold Gorin	1969-1971
Daniel S. Tauman	1971-1973
Melvin Pollack	1973-1975
Laurence H. Tayne	1975-1977
Howard Lidov	1977-1979
Arnold Kaplan	1979-1981
Albert Kopin	1981-1983
Gerald Buckman	1983-1985
Kenneth S. Levin	1985-1987
Howard M. Turner	1987-1989
Morton M. Steinberg	1989-1991
Leonard R. Tenner	1991-1993
Ernest Kaplan	1993-1995
Richard K. Janger	1995-1997
Gerald D. Blumberg	1997-1999
Alan Rutkoff	1999-2001
Karen Kesner	2001-2003
Pearl Kagan	2003-2005
Rodney Slutzky	2005-2007
Lynn S. Schrayer	2007-2009
Steve Abrams	2009-2011
Andrew Brown	2011-2013
Lisa Rosenkranz	2013-2015
Richard Schlosberg	2015-2017
Richard Zelin	2017-

Executive Directors

Bernard N. Klein	1956-1957
Gertrude Resnick	1957-1960
David Weinstein	1962-1963
Cyril Oldham	1963-1971
Mel Karp	1971-1973
Sam Rade	1973-1985
Richard Smith	1985-2001
Kenneth S. Levin	2001-2007
Chuck Kahalnik	2007-2016
Jeffrey T. Baden	2016-

Rabbis

Maurice I. Kliers	1948-1950
Philip L. Lipis	1951-1969
Samuel H. Dresner	1969-1977
William H. Lebeau	1978-1987
Sam Fraint*	1983-1987
Vernon H. Kurtz	1988-2019
Peter Light*	1988-1990
Jay David Sales*	1990-1991
Jay Stein*	1993-1998
David Lerner*	1999-2004
Michael Schwab	2004-
Alex Freedman*	2018-

*assistant or associate rabbi

Educational Directors

Meyer Shisler	1947-1949
Harry Hershman	1949-1957
Louis Katzoff	1958-1971
David Saltzman	1971-1973
Binyamin Markovitz	1973-1977
Marvin Kassoff	1977-1981
Dorothy Wexler	1981-1998
Aaron Klein	1998-2008
Karen Raizen	2008-2011
Alicia Gejman*	2011-
Aliza Drumm**	2011-

* Director of Formal Education
** Director of Informal Education

Cantors

Stanley Martin	1948-1953
Jordan Cohen	1953-1969
Reuven Frankel	1970-1979
Eliahu Treistman	1979-1980
William Weisel	1981-92,94-
(High Holiday Family Service)	
Aryeh Finklestein	1981-1984
Larry Josefovitz	1985-1987
Henry Rosenblum	1987-1998
Larry B. Goller	1998-2015
Benjamin A. Tisser	2015-

Glossary of Hebrew Words and Phrases

Aliyah – Literally "going up," referring to ascending the *bimah* to recite the blessings as part of the reading of the Torah; also refers to moving to Israel to establish residency there.

Aron Kodesh – The ark; the chamber in the front of the synagogue in which the Torah scrolls are stored.

Ashkenaz – The segment of the Jewish people with roots in northern and eastern Europe.

Auf-ruf – Yiddish; the "calling up" of a groom for an *aliyah* before his wedding.

Baal T'kiya – The person who sounds the *shofar*, a ram's horn, during the service on the Jewish new year.

Balabatim – Yiddish; literally the "keepers of the house," meaning the important decision makers in an organization.

Bimah – The platform or stage from which the Torah is read.

Birkat Kohanim – The blessing during certain synagogue services performed by the adults who are members of the priestly class, descendants of Aaron, the first priest.

B'nai Mitzvah – Plural of bar mitzvah, the celebration of a boy's entry into adulthood when he reaches the age of thirteen.

B'not Mitzvah – Plural of bat mitzvah, the celebration of the entry into adulthood by a girl, usually at age twelve or thirteen.

Brit Milah – The ceremony of ritual circumcision.

B'yachad – Together.

Challah – Special bread baked primarily for *Shabbat* and festivals.

198

Chatan B'reisheet – Literally the "Groom of the Book of Genesis," meaning the special honor given to one who has an *aliyah* on the holiday of Simchat Torah.

Chatan Torah – Literally the "Groom of the Torah," another special honor on Simchat Torah.

Chumashim – The books which contain the text of the Hebrew Pentateuch.

Daven – Yiddish; to recite the Hebrew prayers during religious services.

Duchanen – The act of performing *Birkat Kohanim*.

D'var Torah – Literally "a word of Torah," referring to a relatively short teaching covering some aspect of Jewish law or custom.

Eruv – A symbolic enclosure that allows observant Jews to carry needed items in public on *Shabbat*.

Gabai Hagadol – The chief *gabai* at a religious service, the one who coordinates participation by congregants in the service.

Halacha – Jewish law.

Havurah – Fellowship.

Hazzan – Cantor.

Kabbalat Shabbat – The service on Friday evening which commences *Shabbat*.

Kabbalistic – Pertaining to *kabbala*, a mystical school of thought in Judaism.

Kaddish – A prayer extoling the Almighty, recited by mourners at religious services when a *minyan* is present.

Kehila – Community.

Kiddush – The blessing over wine; also refers to the refreshments usually provided after services on *Shabbat* mornings.

Kol Nidre – The evening service which begins the Yom Kippur holiday.

Kol Ha Nearim – Literally the "Voice of the Youth," another special honor on the holiday of Simchat Torah.

Machzor – The special prayer book used on the High Holy Days.

Maot Chitim – The practice of collecting money to enable poor Jewish families to purchase matza for Passover.

Megilat Esther – The Scroll of Esther, read on the holiday of Purim.

Menorah – A seven-branch candelabra.

Mikvah – A ritual bath.

Mincha – The daily afternoon prayer service.

Minyan – The required quorum of ten Jewish adults for conducting public prayers.

Musaf – The additional service recited on *Shabbat*, festivals and other special occasions.

Ner Tamid – The eternal light, usually located above the *aron kodesh* in the synagogue.

Oneg Shabbat – An informal celebration in honor of the Sabbath held on *Shabbat*.

Parochet – The cover, often a curtain, across the front of the *aron kodesh*.

Parshat B'reisheet – The first portion of the Torah.

Perek Yomi – Literally the "Chapter of the Day," referring to the daily study of a specific portion of the Bible.

Pesukei d'zimra – The introductory prayers in the morning service.

Pidyon Haben – The ceremony of redemption of a first born son.

Sepharadit – Pertaining to the customs of the *Sephardim*, Jews with ancestral roots in Spain and North Africa.

Shabbat – The Jewish Sabbath, which runs from sunset on Friday to sundown on Saturday.

Shaliach Tzibur – The "Messenger of the Community," referring to the person who leads the congregation in the Hebrew prayers.

Shiva – The period of mourning following the death of a loved one.

Siddur – A Hebrew prayer book; the plural is *siddurim*.

Siyyum – A ceremony at the conclusion of a significant project.

Slichot – Special prayers for forgiveness recited prior to the Jewish new year.

Sukkot – The plural of *sukkah*, the temporary structure erected for the holiday of Sukkot.

Talitot – Plural of *talit*, a prayer shawl.

Tefilin (also Tephilin) – Known as phylacteries, they are small black boxes containing verses from the Torah and worn during morning weekday services.

Tzedakah – Charity.

Vav – The sixth letter of the Hebrew alphabet, often used to designate the number six.

Yahrzeit – The anniversary of the death of a loved one.

INDEX

203

206

housing, for professional staff, 11-12, 80, 95, 124, 137, 156, 164, 172, 190
HUGS program, 167
Humphrey, Gordon, 22

Illinois Holocaust Museum and Education Center, 165
Impact, 48
Isaacs, Helene, 112, 120
Isaacs, Herb, 104, 112, *146*
Isaacson, Laverne, 92
Isenstein, Samantha, 167, 176
Israel, 29n56, 46, 48, 79, 82-83, 107, 109, 117-118, 125-127, 131, 136-137, 150, 188, 195
Israel Bonds, 29, 33, 46, 79, 81, 109, 125n151, 143-144, 159
Israel Emergency Fund, 83
Israel Scholarship Program, 48

Jack and Mildred Cohen Religious School, 108, 111, 127, 132, 138, 156, 162, 164, 170, 177, 178n193, 181, 184, 192
Jacobson, Rebecca, 194
Janger, Lois, 97
Janger, Richard, 96, 98, 116, 123, 168, 194
Janis, Martin E., 34
Jewish Agency for Israel, 125
Jewish Employment Network, 112
Jewish Federation of (Metropolitan Chicago, 97, 104, 125, 134, 162
Jewish Federations of North America, 124
Jewish National Fund, 125n151
Jewish Theological Seminary, 2, 7, 9, 13, 15, 31, 42, 44, 46, 49n85, 77, 85-88, 100, 104, 112, 113n141, 118, 120, 121n147, 125, 128, 134, 140, 158, 166, 174, 178-179, 190-193
Jewish United Fund, 83, 117
Jewish Youth League, 9
Johnas, Julia, x
Josefovitz, Larry, 98, *154*

Joseph and Mae Gray Cultural and Learning Center, viii-ix, 43n77, *53*, 93, 95, 97, 104, 107n133, 115, 128, 138, 140, 146, 157 158, 162, 165, 172, 182, 191n214
Joseph, Allen, 1, 3, 25n48, *65*
Joseph, Judith, 165
Joy of Judaism Intermarriage Task Force, 111
Jubilee 64 and 65, 43-44
Junior Congregation, 18, 107, 118, 184

kabbalat Shabbat, 81, 112, 123, 133, 137; on the Lake, 133
Kadima group, 107, 124, 165
Kafenshtok, Chuck, 123
Kagan, Joel, 193
Kagan, Pearl, 123, 129, 193
Kaganoff, Ben Zion, 44
Kahalnik, Chuck, 135, 159, 164, 166, 168, 178
Kahn Stage, 33n64
Kahn, Mr. and Mrs. Saul, 33n64
Kamin, Rachel, viii-x, 156, 164-165, 172
Kamin, Sheldon, 44, *68*
Kanes, Dorothy, 84n102
Kaplan, Arnold, 90, *144*
Kaplan, Audra, 165, 178, 182, 188
Kaplan, Bernard, 32n63
Kaplan, Ernest (Ernie), 41, 108-109, 113
Kaplan, Irving, 29, 42
Karp, Mel, 80-81
Kass, Sonia, *76*
Kassof, Marvin, 87, 91
Katz, Betsy Dolgin, x, 121n148
Katz, Cori, 192
Katz, Michael, 89
Katz, William M., 1, 3, 22
Katzoff, Adina, 38, 72, 79
Katzoff, Louis, 31, 34, 35n66, 38-39, 41-42, 72, 79, 84, 86n106, 87
Kaye, Edith, 96, 103
Kaye, Gerald, 47

ABOUT THE AUTHOR

Morton M. Steinberg is Senior Counsel at the international law firm DLA Piper LLP (US). He majored in history at the University of Illinois, graduating with honors in Liberal Arts and Sciences, and received his J.D. from Northwestern University School of Law, where he served as Senior Editor of the *Journal of Criminal Law*. His life-long affiliation with North Suburban Synagogue Beth El began with the synagogue's first nursery school class and continued through Hebrew High School. He later served as secretary and then as president of the congregation. More recently, he has been the synagogue's historian and archivist and continues as a member of its Board of Trustees.

Mort is a trustee of the American Jewish Historical Society, a past president of the National Ramah Commission, and a past member of the Board of Overseers of the Albert A. List College of Jewish Studies at the Jewish Theological Seminary of America. He married Miriam Bernstein Steinberg at Beth El in 1974. They have two children and four grandchildren. They reside in Highland Park, Illinois.

15139256R00129

Made in the USA
Lexington, KY
11 November 2018